Exploring Canada

NEWFOUNDLAND

by Mark Mayell

LUCENT BOOKS®

THOMSON

GALE

San Diego • Detroit • New York • San Francisco • Cleveland • New Haven, Conn. • Waterville, Maine • London • Munich

THOMSON
GALE

Development, management, design, and composition by Pre-Press Company, Inc.

For more information, contact
Lucent Books
27500 Drake Rd.
Farmington Hills, MI 48331-3535
Or you can visit our Internet site at http://www.gale.com

LIBRARY OF CONGRESS CATALOGING-IN-PUBLICATION DATA

Mayell, Mark
  Newfoundland / by Mark Mayell.
    p. cm. — (Exploring Canada)
  Summary: Examines the history, geography, climate, industries, people,
and culture of Canada's Newfoundland.
  Includes bibliographical references and index.
   ISBN 1-59018-048-8 (alk. paper)
  1. Newfoundland and Labrador—Juvenile literature. [1. Newfoundland
and Labrador. 2. Canada.] I. Title. II. Exploring Canada (Lucent Books)
   F1122.4.M395 2003
    971.8—dc21
                              2003002060

Printed in the United States of America

Contents

Foreword

A ny truly accurate portrait of Canada would have to be painted in sharp contrasts, for this is a long-inhabited but only recently settled land. It is a vast and expansive region peopled by a predominantly urban population. Canada is also a nation of natives and immigrants that, as its Prime Minister Lester Pearson remarked in the late 1960s, has "not yet found a Canadian soul except in time of war." Perhaps it is in these very contrasts that this elusive national identity is waiting to be found.

Canada as an inhabited place is among the oldest in the Western Hemisphere, having accepted prehistoric migrants more than eleven thousand years ago after they crossed a land bridge where the Bering Strait now separates Alaska from Siberia. Canada is also the site of the New World's earliest European settlement, L'Anse aux Meadows on the northern tip of Newfoundland Island. A band of Vikings lived there briefly some five hundred years before Columbus reached the West Indies in 1492.

Yet as a nation Canada is still a relative youngster on the world scene. It gained its independence almost a century after the American Revolution and half a century after the wave of nationalist uprisings in South America. Canada did not include Newfoundland until 1949 and could not amend its own constitution without approval from the British Parliament until 1982. "The Sleeping Giant," as Canada is sometimes known, came within a whisker of losing a province in 1995, when the people of Quebec narrowly voted down an independence referendum. In 1999 Canada carved out a new territory, Nunavut, which has a population equal to that of Key West, Florida, spread over an area the size of Alaska and California combined.

As the second largest country in the world (after Russia), the land itself is also famously diverse. British Columbia's "Pocket Desert" near the town of Osoyoos is the northernmost desert in North America. A few hundred miles away, in Alberta's Banff National Park, one can walk on the Columbia Icefields, the largest nonpolar icecap in the world. In parts of Manitoba and the Yukon, glacially created sand dunes creep slowly across the landscape. Quebec and Ontario have so many lakes in the boundless north that tens of thousands remain unnamed.

One can only marvel at a place where the contrasts range from the profound (the first medical use of insulin) to the mundane (the invention of Trivial Pursuit); the sublime (the poetry of Ontario-born Robertson Davies) to the ridiculous (the comic antics of Ontario-born Jim Carrey); the British (ever-so-quaint Victoria) to the French (Montreal, the world's second-largest French-speaking city); and the environmental (Greenpeace was founded in Vancouver) to the industrial (refuse from nickel mining near Sudbury, Ontario, left a landscape so barren that American astronauts used it to train for their moon walks).

Given these contrasts and conflicts, can this national experiment known as Canada survive? Or to put it another way, what is it that unites as Canadians the elderly Inuit woman selling native crafts in the Yukon; the millionaire businessman-turned-restaurateur recently emigrated from Hong Kong to Vancouver; the mixed-French (Métis) teenager living in a rural settlement in Manitoba; the cosmopolitan French-speaking professor of archaeology in Quebec City; and the raw-boned Nova Scotia fisherman struggling to make a living? These are questions only Canadians can answer, and perhaps will have to face for many decades.

A true portrait of Canada cannot, therefore, be provided by a brief essay, any more than a snapshot captures the entire life of a centenarian. But the Exploring Canada series can offer an illuminating overview of individual provinces and territories. Each book smartly summarizes an area's geography, history, arts and culture, daily life, and contemporary issues. Read individually or as a series, they show that what Canadians undeniably have in common is a shared heritage as people who came, whether in past millennia or last year, to a land with a difficult climate and a challenging geography, yet somehow survived and worked with one another to form a vibrant whole.

A Wild, Sea-Dominated Place

The island of Newfoundland was created by the violent collision of ancient landmasses and shaped by the pounding of innumerable North Atlantic storms. Both it and Labrador, the northeastern edge of the Canadian landmass that is the other major section of the province of Newfoundland, were flattened and scrubbed by the huge sheets of glacial ice that periodically covered the land over the past two million years. Newfoundland's cold coastal waters have long been hospitable to fish and marine mammals, but the rocky land, constant fog, and isolated, near-arctic location of the province combine to challenge the survival of all but the hardiest plants and animals, including humans. The land is "the most extensive and dreariest wilderness I have ever beheld"[1] declared naturalist John James Audubon in the early 1830s, after a stay in Labrador to paint its birds.

Yet this wild, sea-dominated place nevertheless has been inhabited by native peoples for thousands of years. It also boasts an early history of Viking exploration and European settlement that rivals any spot in North or South America. Unlike the four original Canadian provinces, Newfoundland rejected union in 1867 in favor of an independence that it held until deciding—in a very close vote—to become a province in 1949. As the site of the easternmost point on North America, Newfoundland has played a historic role in the development of the modern communications and aviation industries. It is also the closest major landfall to the Grand Banks, long world famous for the remarkable, seemingly inexhaustible abundance of cod and other fish.

Canada's Capitals and Major Cities

Within recent years, however, the people of Newfoundland have learned, to their shock and dismay, that fish are indeed an exhaustible resource. With the suddenness of a train wreck, the Grand Banks cod fishing grounds ("fishery") collapsed in 1992 and the Canadian government was forced to ban cod fishing there to allow the cod stocks time to recover. This immediately put tens of thousands of Newfoundlanders who either caught fish for a living or worked in fish processing plants out of work, compounding an already high unemployment rate. Nor has this bust proved temporary—the supply of cod has failed to recover more than a decade later, and stocks of other fish such as flounder have also suffered severe declines. For a society that had depended socially and economically upon fishing for half a millennia, and that relied on Atlantic cod for everything from food to trade, this disaster forced a major reassessment of the provincial character and self-identity.

New Directions

In the long term, the collapse of the cod fishing industry may prove to have a silver lining for Newfoundland. Certainly it has already forced scientists, citizens, and government officials to work more cooperatively to avoid such financial—and environmental—disasters in the future. It has also spurred Newfoundland to consider how it can broaden its economy and make use of some of the other resources the land and seas provide. For example, within recent years Newfoundland has begun to allow energy companies to extract offshore oil in the area of the Grand Banks to develop natural gas resources, and to build hydroelectric stations on Labrador's remote rivers, successfully establishing new industries with reliably in-demand products.

■ *A gun battery on Signal Hill in the foreground overlooks the entrance to St. John's Harbour.*

Provincial officials say that the income from energy exports, as well as from mining, logging, and manufacturing, is needed to help support new initiatives in education, health care, and job training. But the tradeoff is bittersweet for some. Many lifelong residents fear that, as Newfoundland embraces ever more elements of the modern world, those cultural traits that have long given the province its unique flavor and heritage will quickly start to fade. Some native peoples such as Labrador's Innu charge that their rights are being ignored in the rush to exploit the land, and they are not sharing in the bounty. A number of concerned citizens have deep reservations about various industries' potential adverse effects on the province's environment, plants, and animals.

Newfoundland is poised on the edge of an uncertain future. Its people are trying to carve out new and creative ways of living with the rugged natural world, and with the ever-present sea, which remains their physical, historical, and cultural backdrop. The best indication that they are up to this challenge may be the very training in independence and resourcefulness given to them by surviving the rigors of life in Newfoundland.

Geography Is Destiny

N ewfoundland is a stark and picturesque province of rocky shores, deep fjords, and glacially carved alpine plateaus. "Battered by the Atlantic Ocean at Canada's easternmost point," noted *National Geographic* writer Harry Thurston, "it is an elemental place, open to harsh weather, infertile, remote, and watery."[2] Often cold and unforgiving, few who visit it can forget what has been termed its "terrible beauty." The challenging physical environment found throughout Newfoundland, in particular its rough geography, isolated North Atlantic location, and hostile climate, shaped the land and remains a major factor in how its people have been able to make use of natural resources and even to develop socially and economically.

A View from the Air

Unlike Canada's other nine provinces, Newfoundland has a split identity. Its two distinct sections, Newfoundland Island and Labrador, are separated by the narrow Strait of Belle Isle but in many ways are worlds apart. Each has a rugged coastline but otherwise their landscapes and their overall physical characteristics vary dramatically.

Newfoundland Island is a much indented, roughly triangular isle that residents affectionately refer to as "The Rock." Its three sides average about three hundred miles (five hundred kilometers) as the crow flies. This makes it only slightly smaller than the state of Pennsylvania and ranks it as the sixteenth-largest island in the world, larger than Iceland or Ireland.

The Fort Amherst Lighthouse opposite Signal Hill was built in 1952 on the rocky site of a former fort.

"Poised like a mighty granite stopper over the bell-mouth of the Gulf of St. Lawrence," noted Canadian author and naturalist Farley Mowat, "it turns its back upon the greater continent, barricading itself behind the three-hundred-mile-long rampart that forms its hostile western coast."[3] On the island's other two sides it takes refuge from the cold North Atlantic. The Great Northern Peninsula of Newfoundland Island extends farther north than Calgary or Winnipeg, yet the island's eastern Avalon Peninsula is farther south than London or Vancouver. The forty-ninth parallel, the latitude line that forms the border between the United States and Canada from Washington State to Minnesota, just about bisects Newfoundland Island.

Labrador is also roughly triangular in shape but is almost three times the size of Newfoundland Island and lies mostly north of it. Labrador is bounded on one side by the Labrador Sea, an extension of the North Atlantic. Labrador's 5,000-mile (8,000-kilometer) coastline is almost as long as the island's. The area's northernmost point, Cape Chidley on Killenek Island in the Hudson Strait, is only 420 miles (700 kilometers) from the Arctic Circle. To Labrador's south and west is Quebec Province. The 600,000-square-mile (1-million-square-kilometer) landmass bounded by the Hudson Bay, the Labrador Sea, and the Gulf of St. Lawrence is sometimes referred to as the Ungava Peninsula and the Quebec-Labrador Peninsula.

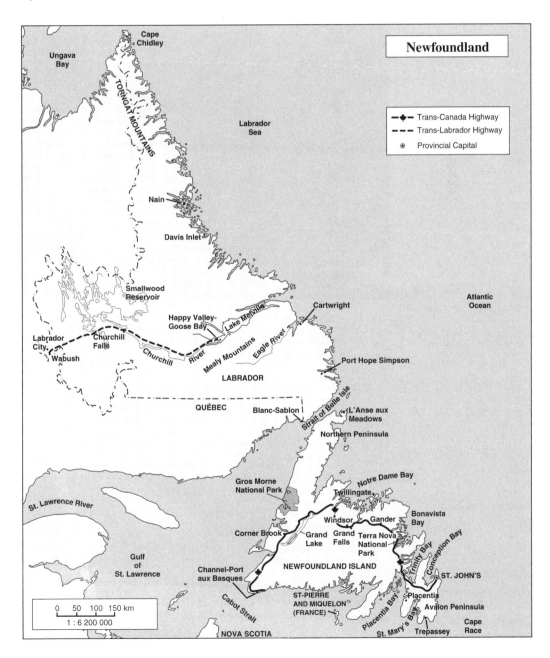

■ *Glaciers carved this freshwater fjord at Western Brook Pond in Gros Morne National Park.*

Newfoundland Island and Labrador differ profoundly in size and location but they share one crucial formative factor: glaciation.

Glaciers Smooth the Way

Over the past 2 million years huge ice sheets have repeatedly covered much of the Northern Hemisphere, including Newfoundland Island and Labrador. These glaciers' actions have been responsible for numerous physical characteristics visible in the province today, from deep scrapes on exposed bedrock to the majestic fjords. Glaciers have also been a major influence on plant, animal, and sea life, and thus human activity as well.

Continental glaciers form when long cold periods allow the amount of snow that falls in the winter to be greater than summer snowmelt. This leads to a greater and greater buildup of snow and ice. The process is self-reinforcing, since snow reflects heat away from the land and discourages melting.

Eventually the top layers of snow compact lower layers into ice. The sheer weight of the resulting continental glacier, which may eventually reach thousands of feet in thickness, causes it to move at a slow but steady pace outward from the glacier's center. The process reverses when gradual warming causes glaciers to melt and retreat.

■ Glacial Effects on Newfoundland's Landscape

Continental glaciers are the "eight-hundred-pound gorillas" of geology, so massive and powerful that they shape mountains and carve coasts. Many of the most prominent and unusual geologic features found throughout Newfoundland were created by continental glaciation. Careful observers may be able to spot not only large-scale effects, like the rounded off tops of the Long Range Mountains on the western coast of Newfoundland Island, but more local features such as the following:

- *Erratics*, like the many that can be seen on the Avalon Peninsula, are large boulders that differ from the underlying bedrock. They often look somehow isolated and out of place. In fact they are out of place: They were picked up by a glacier and carried to a distant spot before being left behind when the glacier melted.

- *Moraines* are ridges, mounds, or sheets of soil, rock, and other debris created at the ends or sides of glaciers, either during a glacier's advancement or from being left behind when a glacier starts to melt and retreat.

- *Striations* are scratches or grooves cut in rocks by other rocks frozen into the underbelly of the glacier as it slowly grinds over the land. Striations thus indicate the direction of movement of a glacier.

- *Whalebacks*, like those in Labrador's Lake Melville, are large, erosion-resistant rocks that tail off smoothly in one direction but have a sharp drop-off on the other, giving the formation a distinct whalelike appearance. Glaciers form whalebacks as they travel in the direction of the "head," smoothing the tail end of the rock while yanking out larger chunks from the other end.

In Newfoundland's highest mountains, the Torngat Range along the northwestern edge of Labrador, you can also observe the effects of mountain, or alpine, glaciers. For example, *cirques* are semicircular, bowl-like depressions left in the side of a mountain by a glacier, and *tarns* are lakes that the glacier carves out at the base of the mountain.

As glaciers advanced and retreated across Newfoundland Island they scoured the surface, rounding the tops of mountains and widening valleys. The massive ice sheets also picked up huge deposits of rock and sediment and, in effect, bulldozed much of the island's soil into the Atlantic Ocean. This displacement of Newfoundland Island's soil would steer the island's history, both by preventing useful agriculture and by helping to form the massive undersea plateau, the Grand Banks, that became one of the world's most bountiful fisheries.

Glaciers also shaped the province's bodies of water. Glaciers deepened the channel between Newfoundland Island and Labrador. When the glaciers receded, springs filled in lowlands and formed ponds and wetlands. Glacially carved inland valleys became the island's three major rivers: the Exploits, Gander, and Humber. The steep-walled coastal bays gouged out by the ice sheets formed Newfoundland's numerous scenic fjords.

Although Labrador was scrubbed in much the same manner as Newfoundland Island, the ice sheets did not sweep away as much of Labrador's topsoil. Some got piled up in moraines at the glaciers' far edges, but much got redeposited to become today's coarse textured soil, which is arable enough for home gardening if not commercial farming. (Some of the latter does occur in the Happy Valley–Goose Bay area.) As on the island, glaciation in Labrador helped to create a rolling landscape pocked with bogs and lakes and veined with rivers, such as the Kanairiktok and Eagle, that flow into the Labrador Sea. The last glacier to cover Labrador, circa twenty thousand years ago, was so heavy that it depressed the land along the coast of the Labrador Sea. When the glacier melted, the sea covered much of the present-day coastline. The land has since rebounded by as much as 450 feet (140 meters) in parts of southern Labrador, pushing the sea back and leaving ancient beaches far from the water.

A Land of Variable Climate

Much like Newfoundland's geography, the province's climate is remarkable for its extremes and local variations. Newfoundland Island, mostly south of Labrador and surrounded by water, is generally warmer and wetter. Labrador, on the other hand, has a climate that is more influenced by the nearby Arctic. Icy winds that come barreling down out of the north can cause freezing temperatures during all but the summer months. Even during the summer, which is typically sunny but short in Labrador, daytime highs average only in the 60s Fahrenheit (15° to 20° Celsius). Winter lows may approach −50° Fahrenheit (−45° Celsius).

The province's weather is also shaped by the Labrador Current, a band of cold water that flows out of the Arctic Ocean into the Davis Strait between Greenland and Baffin Island. The current then runs southeast through the Labrador Sea into the North Atlantic. The frigid air that accompanies the Labrador Current helps keep northern Labrador cold and relatively dry during the winter. It causes coastal waters to be frozen for four months or more, delaying spring. When the cold air over the current collides with the warmer air over the Gulf Stream, the Atlantic Ocean current that flows up the east coast of North America, it causes the area's notorious fogs. St. John's is the foggiest major city in Canada, and some places on the coast of Newfoundland Island get more than one hundred days of fog per year!

■ The Far East of the Western World

Newfoundland stands out as the easternmost point on continental North America. Cape Spear and Cape Race, at the northern and southern ends respectively of Newfoundland Island's Avalon peninsula, are closer to Ireland—approximately eighteen hundred miles (twenty-nine hundred kilometers)—than to western Ontario and are almost twelve hundred miles (nineteen hundred kilometers) east of New York City. The Avalon peninsula is as close to Italy as to parts of British Columbia. If you sailed due south from Cape Race to a point just beyond the Tropic of Cancer, you'd be as close to the west coast of Africa as to Mexico's Yucatan Peninsula. Newfoundland's location on the eastern edge of North America made it an attractive site for the earliest transatlantic telegraphic cables, radio towers, and airplane flights.

■ *The Cape Spear Lighthouse on the outskirts of St. John's is the oldest surviving lighthouse in Newfoundland.*

Island Highlands and Forests

Newfoundland Province spans some nine hundred miles (fifteen hundred kilometers) of latitude from its southernmost to northernmost points, and six hundred miles (one thousand kilometers) of longitude from its easternmost to westernmost points. Thus it should come as no surprise that the environments one encounters at its extremes are vastly different. Ecologists call the region at Labrador's northern tip "low arctic tundra." (*Tundra* is a Russian word for "flat-topped hill.") This is a dry, rocky area totally lacking in tall trees or shrubs.

■ Geology on View at Gros Morne National Park

With its deeply cut inland fjords, rich diversity of arctic and alpine plants and animals, and unusual geologic features, this Newfoundland Island park attracts tourists, hikers, and scientists from all over the world. "What the Galápagos are to biology, Gros Morne is to geology," Britain's Prince Edward remarked upon the opening of the park in 1973. (The Galápagos are a string of islands off the coast of Ecuador that is famous for harboring animals and birds found nowhere else on Earth.)

One of the province's two national parks (the other is Terra Nova on the island's northeast coast), Gros Morne is located about midway up Newfoundland Island's Gulf of St. Lawrence coast. From narrow coastal lowlands the parkland abruptly rises to include an 1,800-foot- (550-meter) high alpine plateau. This plateau is a section of the Long Range Mountains, the northernmost extension of the Appalachian chain that snakes all the way to Georgia in the United States. While not Himalayan in height—Gros Morne ("big lone") Mountain is the park's highest peak at a modest 2,644 feet (806 meters)—they provide awe-inspiring views of steep gorges and azure lakes. Perhaps the single-most-photographed scenic site in the province is the view in the national park of the freshwater fjord at Western Brook Pond.

The park's climate and ecology vary considerably, from temperate woodlands along the coast to tundralike conditions on the exposed mountaintops. As a result visitors can see a unique mixture of plant and animal species—woodland caribou not far from arctic hare, temperate rhododendrons near their arctic cousin the dwarfed Lapland rosebay. Rocks exposed from the earth's interior and ancient ocean fossils are priceless geologic remnants. Such features led UNESCO in 1987 to designate Gros Morne a "World Heritage Site."

■ *Terra Nova National Park on Newfoundland Island features dense forests and pristine ponds.*

At the province's other extreme is the maritime (seaside) barrens of much of the Avalon peninsula, characterized by mostly open heathlands with mixed forest.

Ecologists have identified more than a dozen additional environmental zones, or "ecoregions," in the province. The four most important, however, are the highland forests of Newfoundland Island and the tundra, forest-tundra, and taiga of Labrador.

Much of central Newfoundland Island is a shallow-soiled highland plateau with an elevation of approximately one thousand to two thousand feet (three hundred to seven hundred meters). Patches of forest stand between ridges and hummocks of bare rock. Most of the trees are conifers, such as balsam fir and dwarf black spruce. Aspen and white birch, and small evergreen and deciduous shrubs such as bog laurel, are also represented. Moose, woodland caribou, and arctic hare are able to survive the rough terrain and the cold, snowy winters. Few human settlements have taken root, though mining operations, granite quarries, and logging sites exist.

Labrador: Taiga to Tundra

A very different landscape exists in much of northern Labrador. In the tundra, low year-round temperatures and a lack of winter snowpack (which can help the ground to retain warmth) cause the soil, at varying depths, to be permanently frozen. This permafrost prevents large trees from taking root. The flat plains, buffeted by strong arctic winds, are covered with dwarf shrubs, low-lying herbs, mosses and lichens, and hearty grasses. Caribou herds graze in Labrador's tundra but animal life is limited, especially during the winter. Some native peoples such as the Innu and Inuit have long lived in Labrador's tundra.

Between the tundra and the taiga to the south is a transition zone, the forest-tundra, that can cover hundreds of miles. The forest-tundra has scattered or isolated trees. "I differentiate between taiga and forest-tundra by restricting taiga to be where a red squirrel . . . can travel from tree to tree without having to come down to the ground,"[4] notes ecologist William Pruitt of the University of Manitoba's Taiga Biological Station.

The taiga is the rolling evergreen forest that extends all the way from Yukon Territory to southern Labrador. Another Russian word, taiga originally meant "a marshy forest in Siberia" but now refers to the thick boreal (northern) forest found south of the forest-tundra. In the taiga of Labrador, the soil is not permanently frozen and it snows more. The land can support a variety of trees, especially conifers such as black spruce (Newfoundland's provincial tree) and balsam fir. Beneath the forest canopy you may find blueberry, cloudberry, and other berry-bearing shrubs, a range of mosses and ferns, and small wildflowers. Moderate summer temperatures and rain levels do not make up for the short growing season in the taiga, and the area has typically been used for logging but not farming.

Even within these zones much local variation exists in weather, climate, and geology, yielding interesting and unusual ecoregions such as the limestone barrens in northern Newfoundland Island that are famous for their rare flora.

The Offshore Environment

As an island and a coastal landmass, with most of the human settlement along its coasts, Newfoundland is as much shaped by the sea as by the land. It was a resource of the sea—the Grand Banks—that first attracted Europeans to the area, and it is the sea that remains a major influence on weather, economy, transportation, and more.

The Grand Banks is closely tied to Newfoundland despite the fact that it does not lie within the boundaries of the province. Indeed, the Banks was in international waters until Canada succeeded in enclosing it within a 200-mile (322-

kilometer) exclusive economic zone in 1977. Newfoundland can claim a direct physical connection, however, to the Grand Banks. That is because this bank, or shallow, of the Atlantic southeast of Newfoundland Island was formed from the island's soil, mercilessly scraped and transported by glaciers. The result was the creation of an undersea plateau some 300 miles (480 kilometers) long and 400 miles (640 kilometers) wide.

Sea life is especially abundant at the Grand Banks because of two main factors. First, it is unusually shallow, ranging from about 100 to 500 feet (35 to 185 meters). Because the water is so shallow, sunlight penetrates to the ocean floor and promotes plant growth. Second, the Gulf Stream and the Labrador Current come together over the Grand Banks. The confluence of their warm and cold water promotes conditions favorable for the growth of plankton and other small marine organisms. These provide a key first link in the ocean's food chain and support the vast numbers of larger fish attracted to the Banks, from lobster and crab to cod and halibut.

The diversity of sea life found in the Grand Banks has played a supremely important role in the area's natural and human history. Native peoples fished these waters and hunted the abundant sea mammals, including whales and seals. The Grand Banks lured European fishermen who sailed into the North Atlantic each year to fish what was long one of the greatest cod fisheries in the world. Today, over-fishing has reduced the Grand Banks to a shadow of its former self as a fishery, but the people of Newfoundland have lately begun to

■ A humpback whale breaches out of the water. Humpback, minke, fin, and other whales can often be spotted in Newfoundland's coastal waters.

reap new and unexpected benefits. Organic matter trapped in the rock millions of years ago formed oil, which huge offshore drilling rigs are now extracting.

Land Animals: A Recent and Hardy Bunch

Just as it was for plants, Newfoundland Island was almost a blank slate for animals after the retreat of the most recent glacier. Although Labrador easily became home to a wide range of animal life due to its connection to the rest of North America, reestablishing life on the island was more difficult. Land animals that could not make the tough ten-mile (seventeen-kilometer) swim across the Strait of Belle Isle, or the trek over the frozen sea during the winter, were out of luck. Animals that hibernate during the winter, for example, are still absent from Newfoundland. Thus, no snakes and no frogs.

A relatively limited number of land mammals managed to take up residence on Newfoundland Island before the arrival of European settlers. Various mammal species, including beaver, muskrat, bear, fox, wolf, and caribou, probably traveled across the frozen Strait of Belle Isle during the winter to populate the island's forests. This process is ongoing: Coyote, which have been making a comeback in much of northeastern North America, first appeared on the island in 1987. They apparently crossed from Quebec into the Great Northern Peninsula on winter ice.

In all, only fifteen species of land mammal are native to Newfoundland. Labrador, by comparison, has more than forty native mammals. Biologists consider nine of the island species sufficiently different from their mainland cousins to qualify as distinct subspecies. In recent centuries, humans have also introduced various other species of mammals to Newfoundland Island, including moose (first brought onto the island in 1878 and now numbering more than 120,000, giving the island the highest density moose population in North America), snowshoe hares and, on one offshore island, bison. So far, a few less popular species, like skunks, have been kept off.

The animal that may be the best adapted to Newfoundland's climate and environment is the caribou. Woodland caribou, like those found on Newfoundland Island as well as in southern Labrador, differ only subtly in appearance from tundra caribou, having smaller antlers and a darker coat. The more important distinguishing factor is that woodland caribou favor

■ Tracking the World's Largest Caribou Herd

Labrador is estimated to have thirty times as many caribou as it does people. A single herd of tundra caribou, the George River, that roams northern Labrador during much of the year may be the largest congregation of caribou in the world—a 1993 count estimated 800,000 animals. Newfoundland Island may also contain as many as 100,000 caribou, although these are the more southern woodland caribou.

Huge herds of tundra caribou like the George River can be found in the far northern reaches of much of the Northern Hemisphere, from Canada to Russia. A herd is defined as a group that returns each summer to a specific birthing ground, and it is this area that gives each herd its name. For example, the George River Herd is thought to have returned to the area around the George River in northeastern Quebec for as long as the last two centuries. The Quebec-Labrador Peninsula contains two additional large herds, the Leaf River and Torngat Mountain. Herds of tundra caribou migrate south each winter to graze the expansive plains.

Like woodland caribou, tundra caribou may be feeling environmental pressures, particularly from the reservoirs, dams, and other development that comes with the expansion of the hydroelectric industry. In addition, sport hunting, now a minor industry in Labrador that attracts enthusiasts from afar, is responsible for approximately fifteen thousand caribou deaths annually, substantially more than the numbers taken for subsistence hunting by native peoples. Wildlife biologists observed a much-reduced winter grazing area for the George River Herd in the late 1990s. This suggested that the herd might have declined substantially, perhaps by hundreds of thousands of animals. Almost two centuries of data (going back to fur-trade statistics in the early nineteenth century) and observations, however, document periodic dramatic gains and falls in the caribou population. Early estimates from the latest caribou census, undertaken in the summer of 2001, suggest that the George River Herd has decreased to fewer than half a million animals.

■ *Caribou outnumber people in Newfoundland.*

more forested areas like the taiga and do not migrate each summer and winter.

Both woodland and tundra caribou have adapted well to Labrador but concerns have lately been raised about their long-term survival. A 2000 report by a committee of scientists and government officials said that woodland caribou in Labrador (though not on Newfoundland Island) are likely to become endangered and that as few as 1,750 are now alive there. Factors that may be affecting Labrador's woodland caribou include increased predation from wolves and reduced forest cover from logging.

Most of the animal species known to populate other sub-arctic regions of Canada can also be found within northern Labrador, including arctic hare, foxes, and wolves; woodland and tundra caribou; moose and black bear; and a wide variety of ground animals such as voles, shrews, and mice. The rivers of southern Labrador are home to beaver, muskrat, and river otters as well as abundant salmon, trout, and other fish. Along the coast of the Labrador Sea one may spot seals and whales. Isolated areas in the north harbor polar bears.

Newfoundland's northern climate and relative isolation has affected its domesticated as well as wild animals. Most notably, generations of selective breeding and survival in this difficult environment have led to the development of some famous breeds, including the Newfoundland dog. Early Portuguese fishermen who brought their mountain sheepdogs with them to Newfoundland are thought to have started this breed of large, hard-working water dogs. Today, Newfoundland dogs' thick coats, powerful legs, and webbed feet allow them to survive long swims in cold water. They are said to have pulled many a drowning man from hard seas. Newfoundlands are now equally valued for their intelligence and even temperament. The province's other famous breeds include the Labrador retriever (another superior water dog that was probably developed from the Newfoundland in the area of St. John's) and the Newfoundland pony (a European import circa 1600 that is one of the oldest breeds of domesticated livestock in North America).

A Paradise for Seabirds

Birds' mobility and lower food requirements gave them an edge over land animals in repopulating Newfoundland after the retreat of the last glacier. It was not long before the province was home to a wide variety of owls, jays, woodpeckers, geese, blackbirds, swallows, finches, and sparrows. Today the province harbors more than four hundred species of birds, from raptors to songbirds, including at least ninety in Labrador. The province boasts some of the largest populations in North America of ospreys and bald eagles (in island south coast wilderness areas), razorbills (off the coast of Cartwright in Labrador), and gannets (at Cape St. Mary's Ecological Reserve on the southwestern tip of the Avalon Peninsula).

The marine environment has attracted an even more abundant explosion of seabirds. Numerous commonplace seabirds, such as herring gulls and common terns, frequent the coasts of Newfoundland alongside more exotic black-legged kittiwakes (a medium-sized gull), pomarine jaegers (a large, hawklike bird), and thick-billed murres (a member of the penguinlike auk family). Nature writer and bird enthusiast David A. Snow notes that Newfoundland is home to the world's largest colonies of guillemots, razorbills, and storm petrels. He says:

> The world of our seabirds is rich and chaotic. On the ocean huge feeding flocks, sometimes made up of a dozen or more different species, plunge, swim, or dive after a variety of fish and other small sea creatures. The large breeding colonies of seabirds have been called bazaars due to

■ *The colorful and entertaining Atlantic puffin is Newfoundland's official bird.*

their resemblance to the loud and colourful mix of peoples and cultures found in the bazaars of the Middle East. The Newfoundland and Labrador seabird bazaars are a dazzling mix of sights and sounds.[5]

Newfoundland is also home to North America's largest breeding colony of Atlantic puffins, which the province in 1992 designated its official bird. Atlantic puffins are sometimes called "sea parrots" because of their large and colorful beaks. With their webbed feet, stocky body, and short but powerful wings, they are well suited to swimming and diving in the North Atlantic, where they feed on small fish. They can fly, though only with great exertion, and they tend to land inexpertly, often crashing into fellow birds. Like other puffins, Atlantics return every year to a favorite nesting area, especially islands or grassy cliffs free of predators. Mates nest in burrows that they dig with their beaks and the claws on their feet. Both male and female puffins incubate a single egg and then spend weeks feeding the new chick.

Three islands off the east coast of Newfoundland Island are thought to harbor more than 60 percent of North America's Atlantic puffins. The provincial and national governments have designated preserves and sanctuaries there and elsewhere to protect the birds. Puffin-watching boats that motor out to breeding areas have become a popular tourist attraction in Newfoundland.

A Tough and Resourceful People

The Newfoundland people are a mix of native and newcomer, English and French, Newfoundlanders and Labradorians, who have long shared the struggle to adapt to a demanding North Atlantic environment. They share as well an appreciation of the powerful forces, both on land and in the sea, that have shaped the province they call home. In Labrador, noted writer Robert M. Poole, "People have been involved with the land and sea for so many generations that they cannot imagine life apart from the wild country."[6] Those who have chosen to live here have necessarily had to be a tough and resourceful bunch.

CHAPTER 2

Humanity Comes Full Circle

S uperficially, the landscape of Newfoundland may seem lonely, primeval, almost untouched," notes Harry Thurston. "But beneath the surface lie layers of history and culture."[7] Despite its geography and location Newfoundland has attracted since prehistoric times successive waves of distinct cultures willing to tackle life in a challenging environment. These peoples included not only natives, some of which did not survive competition with later Europeans, but a melting pot of most European nations. The inevitable conflicts nevertheless led to a slowly emerging sense of self-identity by the nineteenth century.

The Earliest Cultures

Labrador and Newfoundland were not inhabited until some time after the retreat of the most recent glaciers, and the earliest people probably came from the spread of nomadic tribes that crossed the frozen Bering Strait into present-day Alaska and slowly spread south and west across the American continents. The earliest inhabitants were known as the Maritime Archaic Nation and may have lived in southern Labrador circa 5000 B.C. Bands of Paleo-Eskimos that came to the area more than two thousand years ago were the forerunners of the Inuit. About five thousand Inuit live in a few villages on the northernmost shores of Labrador to this day.

A number of native ("First Nations") people survived into historic times. The main people on Newfoundland Island from about A.D. 200 until the arrival of Europeans around

■ Shanawdithit: Last of the Beothuk

In 1823 Shanawdithit, her mother, and a sister gave up trying to live with a few other Beothuk in the interior of Newfoundland Island and walked into a small coastal village northeast of present-day Grand Falls–Windsor. Then in her early twenties, Shanawdithit, whom the whites called Nancy, was described as "tall and majestic, mild and tractable, but characteristically proud and cautious" by the St. John's doctor William Carson. Like her mother and sister, Shanawdithit was in poor health, suffering from the effects of starvation. She also had scars from being shot twice. Within a year Shanawdithit's mother and sister died.

During the next six years few other Beothuk followed Shanawdithit's example and voluntarily came to live with whites. Beothuks' experiences with whites were too negative to overcome even the dire circumstances that the last few members of the tribe found themselves in, pushed to the interior of the island and lacking the access to the fish and other coastal resources they needed to survive. By 1827 a thorough search of Newfoundland Island failed to locate a single Beothuk other than Shanawdithit.

Shanawdithit eventually was taken to St. John's and worked as a servant for a number of whites, including the explorer William Cormack and Newfoundland's attorney general James Simms. Cormack recognized her as a unique source of information about her people and helped her document, through stories and drawings, Beothuk practices, traditions, history, and culture. Surprisingly little was known about the Beothuk at the time since they had mostly avoided contact with Europeans after early encounters—the historical record is more or less devoid of references to them for the entire period of 1600 to 1750. Even today almost nothing is known of their spiritual beliefs.

Shanawdithit fell ill and died from tuberculosis on June 6, 1829. Although a few Beothuk living with other tribes may have survived her, for all intents and purposes with Shanawdithit's death the Beothuk became extinct. Her story lives on in Canadian books, movies, and plays, and a plaque in St. John's Church of England Cemetery, where she is buried (the exact site has been lost), commemorates her tragic life.

■ *Shanawdithit was in her late twenties when she died in St. John's.*

1000 and then again in 1500 was the Beothuk, an Algonquin tribe. At their height the Beothuk may have numbered two thousand, organized into small bands of extended families. Before European settlement, the Beothuk were primarily a coastal people, exploiting the sea's rich resources of fish, seals, seabird eggs, and shellfish. The Beothuk probably also went inland periodically for major caribou hunts, since these large animals were important sources of food, clothing, and shelter.

The arrival of European settlers, as well as the more aggressive Mi'kmaq, doomed the Beothuks. The Mi'kmaq are an Algonquin tribe that, prior to the early 1600s, visited southern Newfoundland Island from Nova Scotia during the summer to fish. They were quicker than the Beothuk to adapt to trade with European settlers and eventually helped drive the Beothuk into the interior year-round. The lack of resources there gradually led to the Beothuks' decline. By the early nineteenth century, starvation, disease, and occasional violent incidents with Europeans and Mi'kmaq had decimated the Beothuk. As archaeologist Ralph T. Pastore has noted, "Reduced in numbers, relatively poorly-armed, and lacking in allies, it is perhaps not surprising that the Beothuks ultimately suffered the same fate as the earlier, prehistoric peoples who once lived in Newfoundland."[8]

The other main First Nations group was the Montagnais-Naskapi, a seminomadic Algonquin tribe that survived in the area of the Ungava Peninsula by following the great caribou herds. Caribou and other game provided them with food, clothing, tent covers, tools, and more. Because the Montagnais-Naskapi were not a coastal people, they had less contact with—and competition from—European settlers than did the Beothuks. As a result the Montagnais-Naskapi managed to survive to present times. Approximately two thousand now live in small towns and villages of Labrador, mainly Sheshatshiu and Natuashish. They prefer to be known as Innu, which means "the people" in their language. They refer to their ancestral homeland as Nitassinan, and often find themselves in conflict with provincial plans for highways, dams, and other forms of development.

The Mi'kmaq also survived to the present day. In 1987 the federal government established the Aosamiaji'jij Miawpukek Reserve for a Mi'kmaq band in southern Newfoundland Island, at the mouth of the Conne River. Its population in 2001 was approximately nine hundred. Mi'kmaq communities can also be found in Corner Brook, Benoit Cove, and elsewhere on Newfoundland Island.

A Visit from the Vikings

The first Europeans to see Newfoundland may have been Norse traders aboard a ship that drifted south from Greenland in 986. They did not come ashore but their tales of an unknown land inspired other Norse sailors ("Vikings") to explore the North Atlantic. Around the year 1000, almost five hundred years before Columbus's historic voyages, a Viking ship captained by Leif Eriksson landed on present-day Baffin Island, on Labrador (dubbed Markland, "land of forests"), and then quite probably on Newfoundland Island (named Vinland, for the wild grapes, or possibly berries, they found). They spent a winter on Vinland before returning to the Norse colony on Greenland.

Over the next decade more Vikings visited Vinland. They established a small settlement, now known as L'Anse aux Meadows, on the northernmost tip of Newfoundland Island, which may or may not be the same spot that Eriksson landed at. No more than a dozen or so Vikings probably lived there at a time, in small sod-walled buildings. The site may have been used primarily as a seasonal base camp for fishing and exploring trips, at least one of which reached present-day New Brunswick. After a decade or so the Vikings abandoned it, and Vinland.

The Vikings were also the first Europeans to make contact with native North Americans. A party led by Leif Eriksson's younger brother, Thorvald, came upon a band of natives that were probably Inuits or Beothuks. The Vikings called them *skraelings*, a derogatory term meaning barbarian. "This was a pivotal moment," notes historian Will Ferguson, "not just in Canadian history, but in the history of mankind as a whole. Spilling out of Africa, the human race had pushed north into Europe and east into Asia. The migration had crossed the Bering Strait and spread across North America. And now, on this windswept coast, the two sides had come full circle. It was a reunion as much as it was 'first contact.'"[9]

Ferguson notes that the meeting also set the tone for much of the interaction that would come: The Vikings attacked and killed eight of the natives, with Thorvald also receiving a fatal wound. The Vikings at L'Anse aux Meadows and native peoples did eventually coexist and apparently traded food, clothing, and tools. When the Vikings left around 1010, for unknown reasons, no other European would set foot on Newfoundland for almost half a millennia.

■ Touring L'Anse aux Meadows

The L'Anse aux Meadows National Historic Site is located far off the beaten path, some 650 miles (1,050 kilometers) from St. John's on the tip of the island's Great Northern Peninsula. The land of the thirty-square-mile (eighty-square-kilometer) park is barren and uninviting, with its rocky shoreline, coastal bogs, and stunted trees. The melding of land, sky, and sea can be spectacular, however, especially when a majestic iceberg floats into view.

Those who journey from Deer Lake up Newfoundland Island's northwest coast, along the so-called Viking Trail of Route 430, are rewarded with scenic vistas and interesting villages. Canada Parks has preserved the L'Anse aux Meadows site much as it was when it was discovered by Helge and Anne Stine Ingstad, the Norwegian archaeologists who in the 1960s identified the remains of the eight houses, outbuildings, and workshops as a Viking settlement. Nearby, the parks department has also authentically reconstructed a compound with three full-scale replicas of sod-walled buildings. Visitors who walk into these dark, earthy-smelling buildings can briefly experience what it must have been like to live in the settlement during its decade-long existence as a Viking outpost one thousand years earlier. The "Viking Encampment" also features a half dozen interpreter/actors, clad in authentic Viking clothing and working with Viking tools.

In addition to the archaeological site and Viking encampment, L'Anse aux Meadows has a visitor center with models of Viking ships and displays of artifacts. A few of the artifacts, such as bronze ring-headed pins and soapstone spindle whorls, were excavated nearby. Tools, lamps, swords, and much else have also been collected from other Norse sites. A hiking trail links with nearby bays and lakes. L'Anse aux Meadows is strictly a fair-weather attraction—it is open June through mid-October.

■ *Tourists at L'Anse aux Meadows learn about Viking culture at the entrance to a replica of a sod house.*

Fishermen Are Earliest European Explorers

Newfoundland again eventually attracted the attention of seafaring Europeans for the same reason it was inhabited by the Beothuks: for its closeness to incredibly rich fishing waters. By the late 1400s, large sailing vessels were regularly departing from ports in Portugal, Basque (now a region of northern Spain), and other European locales for months at a time. They would return with their holds full of North Atlantic fish. Many of these boats were no doubt fishing what is now known as the Grand Banks, at the time an incredibly rich fishery teaming with cod. The Grand Banks is located about 100 to 200 miles (160 to 320 kilometers) southeast of Newfoundland, and it is likely that a few of these fishing boats may have landed. If they did, however, it was not to stay but rather only to dry and salt the fish so they would be preserved during the long sail back to Europe. Indeed, this early fish-and-leave lifestyle was to become a model for Europeans on Newfoundland for the next two centuries.

The first post-Viking European to document a landing on Newfoundland was the Italian explorer Giovanni Caboto, who

■ *A seventeenth-century drawing offers a compressed view of how cod were landed, cleaned, split, and laid out for drying in Newfoundland.*

sailed as John Cabot for the British. He and a crew of eighteen were looking for a northern shortcut to Asia when his ship landed in 1497, probably at Cape Bonavista, and claimed this "new found land" for Great Britain. His widely reported claim that in the Grand Banks area one could practically scoop swarming cod from the sea in baskets encouraged other expeditions. Explorers from other countries followed soon after, most notably the Portuguese Gaspar Corte-Real in 1500 and Frenchman Jacques Cartier in 1534. Cartier determined that the land was an island when he sailed through the Strait of Belle Isle.

■ John Cabot's 1497 voyage opened up Newfoundland and the offshore fisheries to Europeans.

Unlike many places much farther south, Europeans were slow to settle on Newfoundland. European rulers granted competing trading and fishing companies "exclusive" rights to Newfoundland's offshore fishery. These companies did not want settlers interfering with the lucrative fishing economy. A number of settlements in the 1600s thus attracted few immigrants, such as George Calvert's colony at Ferryland. It was founded in 1623 but Calvert, also known as Lord Baltimore, left in 1629 to start a colony in a warmer climate. (He eventually helped found Maryland.) A small French colony set up at Plaisance (now Placentia) in the 1620s broke the pattern—it became the French capital of "Terre Neuve," as well as the site of the island's first fort and first permanent military force.

Inevitably, by the late 1600s British and French conflicts over land, harbor, and fishing rights on Newfoundland began to break out in military battles.

The Battle for Dominance

One of the deadliest battles between the British and French occurred on the Avalon peninsula in 1696–1697. A French force of four hundred soldiers attacked and destroyed a string of English settlements south of St. John's. In the winter of 1696 the French reached St. John's, defended by fewer than one hundred British citizens. The locals put up a ferocious fight but the French overwhelmed them and went on

■ *A sketch shows the fortified entrance to St. John's Harbour, circa late eighteenth century, looking out to the sea.*

to destroy other British settlements on the peninsula before returning to Placentia. The British were forced to respond militarily, notes historian Bernard Ransom:

> This signal disaster, and especially the consternation it caused in New England, at last stimulated the British government to provide a permanent defence force for the island. A strong British relief force of 1500 troops reoccupied St. John's in the summer of 1697: they found the town abandoned, pillaged and every building destroyed. The following year construction was begun on a well-engineered fortification—Fort William—which, when completed in 1700, had brick-faced ramparts, bomb-proof parapets, powder magazines and proper barracks.[10]

Finally aroused to the urgency of the situation, the British military won a number of decisive battles over the next decade. In 1713 the French were forced to sign the Treaty of Utrecht, formally ceding control over Newfoundland to the British. The French did retain the right to fish on the west coast of the island, a right they kept until 1904.

Long-term British supremacy was not to be so easily won, however. The pattern was repeated again in the Seven Years' War of 1756–1763. Britain eventually prevailed on the field of battle and forced France to sign another face-losing treaty, the Treaty of Paris, in 1763. The French basically lost all of their

New World colonies, with the exception of two small islands, St. Pierre and Miquelon, off the southern coast of Newfoundland. These islands remain French possessions to this day.

Although political control over Newfoundland was finally secured by the British, the area remained sparsely settled. It was still predominantly a base for fishermen whose ties were to their European homelands.

A Brief Heyday of Immigration

Newfoundland's relatively homogenous population is due to a spurt of European migration it experienced around 1800. At the time the offshore cod fishery, after decades of steady growth, began to level off. The national animosities generated by the Napoleonic Wars, and the increased activity of pirates, also made fishing the Grand Banks more dangerous. These developments encouraged year-round settlement of Newfoundland.

Many of the newcomers began to work the so-called inshore fisheries (as opposed to the offshore Grand Banks fishery). Other settlers took part in the growing sealing industry. By the early 1830s Newfoundland sealers, working out of ships

■ *Seal hunters perch everywhere aboard a sailing steamer amid Newfoundland coastal icefields, circa 1880s.*

that sailed to the edge of the seasonal sea ice in the spring, were killing as many as six hundred thousand seals per year.

The greatest number of immigrants arrived in 1814–1815, when some eleven thousand mostly Irish emigrants sailed into St. John's. This wave of immigration had subsided by the 1840s and relatively few newcomers settled in Newfoundland after that. This meant that by the mid-twentieth century more than 90 percent of the population had been born in Newfoundland.

St. John's grew as a trade and distribution center, shipping salt cod and seal skins to Europe, the Mediterranean, South America, and beyond. Its population swelled from 3,000 in 1800 to 30,000 by 1857 (out of a total Newfoundland population of 124,000). According to Newfoundland historian Shannon Ryan:

> St. John's became truly the capital of Newfoundland, and the growth of a large more or less resident middle class led to the development of social and political consciousness which resulted in the formation of groups and institutions devoted to charitable, social and eventually political ends. This middle class became the ruling elite of the Island and took the lead in the definition of a distinct Newfoundland consciousness, which was first expressed in the desire for internal self-government.[11]

As was the case in Newfoundland, the earliest settlers in Labrador were isolated pockets of cod fishermen in the seventeenth and eighteenth centuries who began to stay year-round rather than just seasonally. Many of these fishermen were French, which eventually led to a short-lived (1774–1809) claim of Quebec control over the area. During the early nineteenth century, larger concentrations of European missionaries and immigrants began to settle along the coasts of Labrador, much to the dismay of both the Inuit and the Montagnais-Naskapi. A Moravian missionary set up in Nain in 1771 was the most permanent European incursion (the building that remains there today is one of the oldest in northern Canada), followed by some minor Hudson's Bay Company activity in the early 1800s. The powerful fur-trading company sponsored a number of exploratory expeditions but could not duplicate the profitable trade network it had established in western Canada. By the 1840s it was barely active in Labrador, though the intermarriage of its fur traders with native women led to the small Métis (French for "mixed") population still found in Labrador today.

■ Irish Bays and French Shores

Settlement patterns from the early eighteenth century have left their mark on modern-day Newfoundland. The island's largest bays, such as Conception, Trinity, and Placentia, have unique cultural identities that can be traced to settlers' heritage. The same is true for its "shores," such as the French Shore and the Southern Shore. People tended to work with and interact more with the people of their own bay, reachable by boat travel, than with other communities perhaps closer by land but not connected by roads. In addition, when new settlers arrived they tended to congregate with others from their homeland, or with those of the same religion. Thus, St. Mary's developed as the Roman Catholic bay and Trepassey as the Irish bay. The west coast of Newfoundland Island, which came under full Newfoundland control only in 1904, was long fished and settled by the French and goes by the name the French Shore to this day. Placentia Bay, for more than a century the site of the French capital of Newfoundland, also retains its French influence. The vast majority of the immigrants who settled the Trinity, Bonavista, and Notre Dame bays of the northeast island coast were from the four British counties of Wessex.

"In addition to Newfoundlanders feeling an attachment to their communities," notes Jeff A. Webb of the Newfoundland and Labrador Heritage website, "they sometimes felt some sense of belonging to a larger 'community' of their bay. One might hear people describing themselves as 'Placentia Bay men' or 'Placentia Bay women' for example. Those who had moved to urban centres were often the strongest in their identification with their home bay and community."

■ *A French fishing station is poised on Newfoundland's western shore in 1844.*

■ *An early drawing de-picts various aspects of Atlantic coastal whaling, which the Basques and others were doing off the shores of Labrador from the 1550s onward.*

Expansion and settlement in Newfoundland and Labrador began to create pressure for more effective, and more local, control over the area's finances and government. The people increasingly wanted the type of self-government that Britain had already granted Newfoundland's coastal neighbors, Nova Scotia and Prince Edward Island.

A Semi-Independent Country

In the early 1800s, Patrick Morris, an Irish-born merchant, and Dr. William Carson, the scribe for Shanawdithit, were the chief agitators for a representative government for Newfoundland. In 1824 Britain allowed Newfoundland to choose a governor and eight years later the British parliament permitted the island to establish a two-house legislature, with one of the houses having popularly elected representatives. It was not until 1855, however, that Newfoundland won from Britain the right to be self-governing concerning local matters, and the right to control its own finances. The people elected Philip Little as their first premier. This meant that Newfoundland was the last of Great Britain's North American colonies to achieve self-government. Great Britain retained control, however, of Newfoundland's foreign affairs, an often-uncomfortable compromise that would limit Newfoundland's development.

The Newfoundland government took immediate steps to liberate the economy from its overreliance on the offshore fishery. Much effort was put into expanding the island's small farming industry, with the formation of agricultural societies. The amount of land under cultivation expanded quickly but most farms remained small and less productive than those with better soil and a longer growing season in, for example, southern Ontario. In the early 1860s Newfoundland entrepreneurs also opened the island's first copper mine. The worldwide demand for cod remained strong, and Newfoundland seem to be poised for self-sufficiency just at the time when they faced a major decision: whether to accept membership in the new country of Canada.

Newfoundland to Canada: Drop Dead

In 1864 delegates from Newfoundland, Ontario, Quebec, Nova Scotia, and New Brunswick met to consider the merits of forming a confederation that would be independent from Great Britain. The five British colonies quickly resolved to pursue independence, but in 1865 Newfoundland determined that an election, rather than an act of the legislature (which the other colonies were planning to use), would be needed to decide whether it would join the confederation. Thus, when the new country of Canada was born on July 1, 1867, after an official act of the British Parliament, Newfoundland was not included. It needed to hold an election, which was scheduled for November 1869. The premier at the time, Frederick Carter, took a pro-confederation position. The leader of the anti-confederates was Charles Fox Bennett, a prominent and extremely wealthy St. John's merchant. Many other merchants were also against confederation, saying that it would result in people and businesses having to pay high taxes to Canada.

The pro-confederation forces could not counter this appeal to Newfoundlanders' independent streak. The vote was not even close—confederation was rejected overwhelmingly. As a popular song of the time went, "Cheer up, my gallant countrymen, The fight is fought and won. Confederates are routed, And beaten two to one."

As historian J.K. Hiller has noted, "The election showed clearly that most Newfoundlanders were strongly opposed to confederation. If it was a vote of no-confidence in Canada, it was also a vote of confidence in Newfoundland, an assertion

■ *St. John's businessman and politician Charles Fox Bennett led the drive against confederation in the late 1860s.*

of confidence that the colony had the resources to survive and prosper on its own."[12] This rejection of confederation would not be reversed for eighty years, although much sooner than that Newfoundland came to realize that its dream of political and economic independence would be difficult to achieve.

Undercurrents of Trouble

In the decades to follow, Newfoundland chafed under the control still exerted to some extent by the British. Newfoundland also experienced conflicts over trade and other issues with neighboring Canada, which not surprisingly resented its rejection of confederacy, and with the United States. These undercurrents of trouble would become more prominent as Newfoundland experienced a series of physical and financial disasters as it struggled to become more self-sufficient entering the twentieth century.

The Struggle for Self-Sufficiency

CHAPTER

3

F rom the early 1800s to the present Newfoundland's physical isolation and reliance on fishing have gradually dwindled in importance as factors that determine its political and social identity. Much of the history of the province during the twentieth century and into the twenty-first has been determined by its location, both isolated and close to Europe, and by its growing need to develop an economy less reliant upon fishing.

The Golden Age of Cod Fishing

Newfoundland's fishery reached a notable peak in the 1870s and 1880s, accounting for more than 90 percent of the country's annual exports and employing more than half of the population. Fishermen were enjoying high world prices, and dried salt cod was being exchanged for imports from Britain, the United States, and Canada. Meanwhile, the population of Newfoundland had reached 200,000 people.

Even as this golden age existed, its limits were being hinted at by new developments. Chief among these were steam powered ships and the advent of refrigeration. These new technologies would dramatically change the nature of cod fishing in the twentieth century, and in doing so swing the advantage from cod's remarkable reproductive and survival abilities to humanity's remarkable fish-killing abilities. As Mark Kurlansky notes, "Once motor ships replaced sail and oar, fishing no longer had to be done with 'passive gear'—equipment that waited for the fish. Fish could now be

■ *Drying fish dominated the St. John's waterfront during the 1890s.*

pursued. And since a bigger, more powerful engine could always be developed, the scale of the fishing could increase almost limitlessly."[13] Refrigeration also sped huge catches to markets, allowing ships to return to the fishery much quicker. It would take a century before the ultimate victor would become apparent in this struggle between cod and humanity, but it was a fight that the cod was destined to lose.

Disasters Disrupt Security

A series of sobering disasters in the 1890s also added to Newfoundland's growing sense of insecurity. The most tangible disaster was a major fire that destroyed most of St. John's on July 8, 1892. For the previous month the city had received little rain, and when a stable caught fire from a dropped smoking pipe, strong winds and low pressure in fire mains spelled disaster. Many of the city's shingle-roofed wooden buildings were left in ashes, and the fire became so strong that even many stone and brick buildings were gutted. Twelve hours later much of St. John's had become smoldering ruins. As many as half the buildings in the city were destroyed, and some eleven thousand residents were left homeless, though only three died. Only about a third of the $13 million in property losses were insured, and the economy was not large enough for the financial devastation to be ignored.

Two years later, as a direct result of the St. John's fire, Newfoundland experienced a series of bank failures that put a further damper on development. When a downturn in the price of fish came at the same time, there was a flurry of talk about whether Newfoundland should reconsider confederation. The province weathered the storm, however, and went on to experience a temporary prosperity during the first two decades of the twentieth century. The fishing industry recovered, and a railway completed in 1898 between St. John's and Channel-Port aux Basques boosted various businesses. Newfoundland encouraged foreign investors to pump money into the small land-based economy, leading to growth of the railway and mining industries. In 1908 the first newsprint mill opened. As the Newfoundland and Labrador Heritage website notes, "Standards of living rose, and the Government of Newfoundland was treated by London on an equal footing with the larger Dominions of the British Empire, such as Canada."[14] The decades after 1900 also saw Newfoundland play a prominent role in the new communications and aviation industries, mainly due to its location on the easternmost point of North America.

■ *Much of St. John's was a smoldering ruin after the fire of 1892.*

Bridging the Gap to Europe

Newfoundland's proximity to Europe made the St. John's area a favorite takeoff and landing site for early twentieth-century record-breaking aviators. The very first transatlantic flight took off from St. John's Lester's Field on June 14, 1919, piloted by

■ "The Fish That Changed the World"

The lifeblood of Newfoundland until a decade ago was a remarkable fish that, according to its chronicler Mark Kurlansky, author of the 1998 book *Cod: A Biography of the Fish That Changed the World*, hastened Europeans' exploration of North America, shaped the history not only of Newfoundland but much of northeastern North America, and even spurred the American Revolution.

The cod is capable of such achievements for a number of reasons. It can grow to fifty pounds (twenty kilos), survives quite nicely in the extreme cold of the North Atlantic, rarely catches any diseases, and will eat almost anything. "It swims with its mouth open and swallows whatever will fit," Kurlansky says in his book, "including young cod." It is also easy to catch, often biting unbaited hooks and then not putting up much of a fight. Its fresh meat is almost fat free yet high (18 percent) in protein. The lack of fat makes cod eminently preservable by means such as drying and salting, in which case it is one of the most concentrated sources of protein known to humanity. In the days before refrigeration, such a trait made cod one of the most widely traded foods in the world.

"If ever there was a fish made to endure," Kurlansky goes on to say, "it is the Atlantic cod—the common fish. But it has among its predators man, an open-mouthed species greedier than cod."

■ *Large cod like this were once common on the Grand Banks.*

John Alcock and Arthur W. Brown. After a sixteen-hour, 1900-mile (3,000-kilometer) flight in their twin-engine biplane, they survived a rough landing in an Irish peat bog.

Charles Lindbergh's first transatlantic solo went from New York to Paris in 1927, but Newfoundland was the takeoff site for the first woman's (and only the third-ever) solo transatlantic flight. It was accomplished on May 20, 1932, by the daring American pilot Amelia Earhart. She left from Harbour Grace, across Conception Bay from St. John's, flying a single-engine Lockheed Vega. She landed in a field near Londonderry in northern Ireland fifteen hours later. The accomplishment made Earhart world-famous and universally grieved when, five years later, she and navigator Frederick Noonan disappeared over the Pacific Ocean in an attempted around-the-world flight. (The best current evidence suggests that Earhart and Noonan crash-landed on remote Gardner Island and perhaps even survived for a few weeks before dying.) Newfoundland commemorates its aviation history at the Conception Bay Museum at Harbour Grace, not far from where the historic runway strip is still visible, and at the North Atlantic Aviation Museum in Gander.

■ *American aviatrix Amelia Earhart stands in front of her Lockheed Vega two days before setting out on the first transatlantic solo flight by a woman in 1932.*

St. John's was also well situated to play a prominent role in the fast expanding communications industry. The first successful transmission of a telegram by transatlantic undersea cable, on August 17, 1858, was through a cable that was laid on the ocean floor from Newfoundland to Valentia, on the west coast of Ireland. This first transatlantic cable was technologically primitive and it quickly failed—after only a month its poor insulation and manufacturing faults in its construction left it dead in the water. Successors built from the mid-1860s onward, however, mostly from England to St. John's (and then across the island and south to the rest of North America), were reliable and highly profitable by 1900.

■ Marconi's Famous Transatlantic Message

On December 12, 1901, Guglielmo Marconi pressed a telephone headset to his ears as he sat in an abandoned hospital not far from the cliffs of today's Signal Hill, St. John's. He was listening intently for a radio signal originating some 1,700 miles (2,735 kilometers) away in England. When he finally heard the faint "pip pip pip" of the Morse code for the letter *S*, he was the first person to experience a technology—long-distance wireless telegraphy—that would revolutionize the communications industry.

Marconi was barely twenty-one in the mid-1890s when he left his native Italy for Great Britain, which offered more hope for official support of his groundbreaking work on wireless telegraphy. By 1897 he was manufacturing radio sets that could transmit and receive Morse code over short distances. This promised great advantages for ship-to-ship communication, but scientists at the time thought that radio signals would be limited in the distance they could travel by the curvature of the earth. Beyond a hundred miles or so, it was thought that the signals would fly off in a straight line into space. Marconi proved otherwise (scientists now know that radio signals bounce off the upper atmosphere and return to Earth), and his technology quickly came into direct competition with telegraphic cables.

Marconi's achievements in telegraphy, radio, and other technologies won him worldwide fame, considerable wealth, and a Nobel Prize for Physics before his death in 1937. His work is commemorated at Cabot Tower, built in 1897 and now a popular landmark in the Signal Hill National Historic Site at the entrance to St. John's Harbour. Although the tower has not been used for signaling since 1960, it features a number of exhibits relating to Marconi's wireless innovations.

■ *Radio pioneer Guglielmo Marconi is shown here in St. John's shortly after his historic first transatlantic radio transmission in December 1901.*

The most stunning scientific achievement to occur in Newfoundland at this time was Guglielmo Marconi's first demonstration of transatlantic wireless telegraphy, using an aerial held aloft over St. John's Signal Hill by a kite. Despite

Newfoundland's central role in the development, however, the province was slow to benefit. This is because it had signed an exclusive fifty-year agreement with the powerful Anglo-American Telegraph Company in 1854. The agreement prevented Newfoundland from allowing Marconi, or anyone else, from setting up a telegraphic facility on the island until 1904. Anglo-American unleashed its lawyers on Marconi soon after his first experiment, prompting the Canadian government to help Marconi set up a wireless telegraphy station on Cape Breton Island, Nova Scotia. Marconi did return to Newfoundland after 1904 to set up a wireless station at Cape Race.

Newfoundland's Ship of State Founders

Despite the presence of industrial pioneers like Marconi, Newfoundland's already struggling economy went into a death spiral after World War I. The price of fish fell, causing the percentage of the fishery that accounted for exports to shrink from 71 percent in 1920 to 37 percent in 1930. Money spent on the war increased the country's already high public debt, built up from expenditures on railroad building and expansion of farming. Newfoundland's small tax base also made financial reforms difficult. Politicians engaged in fierce debates but none seemed to have any practical solutions for the country's prolonged economic recession. When the Great Depression started in the early 1930s, industries shut down and residents left in droves. By the mid-1930s it is estimated that more than 15 percent of native-born Newfoundlanders had moved out of the country.

In 1932 the government was faced with a difficult choice. What was left of its revenue after payments were made to thousands of poor people had to be spent on servicing the country's debt. Most of this almost $100 million debt was owed to a group of Canadian banks. When these and other banks refused to make any further loans, Newfoundland was essentially bankrupt. In 1934, the huge debt and the widespread lack of confidence in political leaders led the people of Newfoundland to accept suspension of its semi-independent government in favor of temporary rule by a London-appointed commission.

It would be another fifteen years before Newfoundland regained a measure of self-rule. The economy, even with British aid helping to pay off the national debt, was slow to recover. It was not really until World War II started that Newfoundland began to stand on its own feet. Again, its location

■ Nazi Germany Invades the Province

Being the far east of North America has its advantages in peacetime but it also made Newfoundland somewhat vulnerable to German attack during World War II. In fact a German submarine, U-537, made the only armed Nazi landing on North American soil when it came ashore near Cape Chidley, Labrador, in October 1943.

In less than a day the German troops successfully set up an antenna mast, wind vane, battery-operated radio transmitter, and other equipment on a tripod. It was a fairly sophisticated, for its time, automatic weather station, capable of sending U-boat headquarters regular "radio weather-grams." Because Atlantic weather patterns often originated in the west, this early data on factors such as temperature, windspeed, and humidity was valuable ship-hunting intelligence. For reasons that remain unclear, after about two weeks of periodic transmissions the station's signal was jammed and became useless to the Germans. U-537 was sunk and all its sailors killed in 1944, leaving few people alive with any knowledge of the weather station's existence.

The site of the weather station is so remote that Canadian officials did not learn of it until the early 1980s, when a German engineer writing a history of the German weather service came across some old records and queried a Canadian army historian about the station's fate. The response from Canada was basically, "What are you talking about?" A Canadian coast guard ship sent to investigate found the site, still with much of its original equipment, although Inuit hunters had apparently used some of the equipment for target practice.

Newfoundland also experienced more deadly enemy activity during World War II when a Nazi U-boat sank a Nova Scotia-to-Newfoundland ferry, the *Caribou,* off Channel-Port aux Basques on October 14, 1942, at a loss of 136 lives. German submarines also sank four ship in Conception Bay that fall.

■ *A badly damaged German U-boat surrenders to seamen from the Royal Canadian Navy corvette* Chilliwack *in March 1944 in the North Atlantic.*

was a factor: The United States signed an agreement with the British government to build three military bases in Newfoundland and Labrador, for use as staging grounds for sending planes and armaments to Europe. The many servicemen that worked at these bases further pumped up the local economy. An increase in the price of fish and other exports also helped to make Newfoundland more financially stable.

Unfortunately, the war proved a temporary respite and Newfoundland's underlying troubles were quick to resurface after 1945.

Independence or Confederation?

Newfoundland's residents faced a difficult choice in the late 1940s: Should Newfoundland once again pursue political independence, even though its long-term economic history seemed to suggest this was an elusive notion, or should it become a province of Canada? The landmark 1949 referendum that decided the issue in favor of confederation passed by the smallest of margins, with much of the credit for its passage going to Joey Smallwood, the dominant figure in late–twentieth-century Newfoundland politics. After Newfoundland became Canada's tenth province on March 31, 1949, Smallwood reigned as its premier until 1972.

Smallwood flirted with a political career but had lost his only election, as a Liberal Party candidate for a seat in the provincial legislature in 1932, and was working as a pig farmer in Gander when the post–World War II confederation debate presented him with a choice opportunity to shine. In newspaper columns and radio appearances, he quickly became the foremost proponent of union with Canada. He was elected as a delegate to the National Convention of 1946 that was formed to make recommendations to the public and was arguably the most influential voice that led to the slim vote in favor of provincehood in the second public referendum of 1948. He was the natural choice for appointment as interim premier in 1949, and he won the first election as a Liberal later that year.

Welcome to Canada

Newfoundland's first few decades as a Canadian province were characterized by lofty promises of land-based industrial development that went mostly unfulfilled. The promised

■ *Citizens in Corner Brook read about Canadian prime minister Mackenzie King's reaction to Newfoundland's July 1948 pro-confederation vote.*

federal subsidies that convinced many Newfoundlanders to accept provincehood kept Newfoundland going, but most of Smallwood's attempts to promote industrialization failed. One notable economic guru he hired embezzled public money. A program he instituted that "resettled" natives and residents of outposts in more urban "growth centers" was controversial, with critics saying it destroyed local culture and disrupted the fishing economy. Even the most prominent scheme that succeeded, the Churchill Falls hydroelectric project, was dogged by charges of insensitivity to cultural and environmental concerns.

In accepting provincehood, Newfoundland had agreed that Canada would take over control of a number of public functions, such as banking. But Canada also took over control of the fishery, a development that many of the people of Newfoundland, and especially its fishermen, would come to regret.

The Collapse of the Cod Fishery

As a place that long depended upon seemingly limitless supplies of fish, Newfoundland experienced total shock and

■ "Father of Confederation" Joey Smallwood

Joey Smallwood was born in Gambo in northeast Newfoundland Island in 1900. He grew up poor in St. John's and after high school became a printer's apprentice and then a fledgling reporter. He left Newfoundland briefly to work for a leftwing paper in New York City but by 1925 had married and returned to his homeland for good. For the next twenty years he worked as a labor organizer, journalist, and radio broadcaster, slowly gaining recognition as a voice of the common working person.

Smallwood's successful campaign in favor of confederation led to his election as Newfoundland's first provincial premier. He used his popularity as premier for more than twenty years to promote a number of still-controversial policies, particularly the attempt to resettle the residents of hundreds of small coastal communities ("outports") into newly formed industrial centers. These policies gained him both friends and foes. The Canadian naturalist Farley Mowat offered this blistering attack in *The Rock Within the Sea*: "'Off with the old and on with the new' is his guiding principle, and he has applied it with a vigour and a haste that have made no reckoning of the psychic and spiritual havoc it has created in the lives of his own people." Others praised Smallwood's willingness to present difficult truths to the electorate, as when he backed confederation by declaring, "We are not a nation. We are a medium-sized municipality . . . left far behind the march of time."

Smallwood was in his mid-seventies when he ended his political career but he was too energetic to retire. Instead he added a final notable chapter to his life, undertaking the writing and editing of the ambitious *Encyclopedia of Newfoundland and Labrador*. The first two volumes were in print by the time Smallwood died at age ninety in St. John's. The Joseph R. Smallwood Heritage Foundation finished the project, now an authoritative, five-volume, thirty-nine-hundred-page resource that is Canada's only provincial encyclopedia. It is a fitting memorial to a man for whom Newfoundland was all.

■ *Joseph Smallwood signs the "Terms of Union" document on December 11, 1948.*

dismay—and widespread unemployment—when the un-thinkable occurred in 1992: The world-famous stocks of cod in Newfoundland's waters reached near commercial extinc-tion, seemingly almost overnight. But, of course, the warning signs had been quite visible for some time, even as Canadian and Newfoundland officials chose not to see them.

It became apparent to Canada during the 1950s and 1960s that inland industries were not a cure-all for Newfoundland's chronic economic problems. The government then focused its attention on Newfoundland's prime natural resource: its in-credible Grand Banks fishery. The most immediate problem was gaining greater political control over the Grand Banks, which Canada finally did in 1977 by extending its exclusive fishing rights to 200 miles (322 kilometers). Canada argued it needed this to prevent huge trawlers from Russia, Japan, and other countries from taking too many fish from the Grand Banks. Unfortunately, once these foreign ships no longer pa-trolled the Grand Banks, Canada's own supertrawlers came in with a vengeance. Canada's intention was to industrialize the offshore cod fishery, which it did during the 1980s. Cod were treated as an inexhaustible resource, and modern technology along with huge, fine-meshed nets allowed trawlers to find, catch, and process them relentlessly.

Finally, in 1992, the stock of northern cod proved to be not inexhaustible at all. Some, mostly small, cod could still be found, but nowhere near enough for them to be fished com-mercially. The Canadian government was forced to announce a moratorium on fishing for northern cod. Some thirty thou-sand Newfoundlanders, including those who both caught and processed the fish, were out of work.

Given how important fishing had been to Newfoundland for more than three centuries, the repercussions on people and communities were widespread. As the Newfoundland and Labrador Heritage website has noted:

> The Newfoundland of the present is the product of a com-plex and distinctive sequence of events, and for most of that history, the fishery has been central. Although for most of the 20th century it has not been the most signifi-cant money-earner in the economy, it has retained a cen-tral place in the culture, and has continued to be the main, and in some cases the only, support of hundreds of rural communities. With the collapse of the cod-fishery in 1992, many of those rural communities are in crisis. Newfound-land's survival is in the balance.[15]

Daily Life

I n many respects Newfoundland remains a remote and isolated place, connected in some ways more closely to England than to the rest of Canada—or to the United States, considering the difficulty and expense of the drive-and-ferry access to the island. Many aspects of the peoples' lifestyles, from traditional foods to art forms, can be traced to English or European influences yet are not common in other places in Canada. Increasingly, however, the remnants of the past are giving way to the pressure of the new, and the transformations in business, health, education, and recreation that the province is experiencing are drawing it closer in substance and style to modern North American norms.

Exploring Newfoundland's Largest City

St. John's is by far Newfoundland's most dominant city, serving as the province's political capital as well as its business, financial, and cultural center. It has grown in recent years and has now meshed into an urban sprawl with neighboring Mount Pearl, one-sixth its size but still the next largest city in the province. (The only other city in the province is Corner Brook, which grew on the basis of its many paper mills.)

Most of the 175,000 or so residents of the St. John's metropolitan area lead lives typical of city dwellers throughout North America, although in a locale with relatively little pollution, racial strife, or crime. Many workers commute from Mount Pearl into St. John's to work in the government, communications, or transportation industries. St. John's is also a working seaport, thanks to its location as the easternmost city in North America and its sheltered, deep-water harbor. The waterfront combines the activities of a busy commercial shipping port with tourist-oriented sites, including whale- and iceberg-watching boats. Within the past few years St. John's has become a cruise ship destination, with seventeen ships carrying ten thousand visitors making port calls in 2001.

St. John's is a charming and historic city full of museums, art galleries, craft stores, and shopping emporiums. Visitors should not be deterred by the climate, notes *Maclean's* magazine writer Anthony Wilson-Smith:

> Go to St. John's in the middle of a cold, dark, damp February, and you wonder how anyone could live there year-round. But by mid-May, the streets are alive, and the old wooden buildings show to best advantage—St. John's is among the great undiscovered cities of the world. That latter quality is changing: these days, the arts and craft stores on funky Water Street have a sophisticated array of products and visitors.[16]

St. John's is one of the oldest cities on the continent—dozens of ships were anchored in its harbor at least forty years

■ A Quirky Time Zone

Newfoundland residents and businesses face an unusual challenge in adapting to a time zone that is a half hour, rather than the customary full hour, ahead of or behind neighboring time zones. The quirky time zone is Newfoundland Standard Time (NST), which is used on Newfoundland Island and on a northcoast sliver of Labrador. NST is three hours and thirty minutes behind Greenwich Mean Time, the international starting point for time established by international convention in 1884.

Newfoundland established NST with an act passed in 1935, well before it joined Canada. Government officials felt that it was appropriate because Newfoundland Island is situated betwixt and between—too far east for Atlantic Standard Time and too far west for Greenland Standard Time, which includes a part of Greenland to the north and eastern Brazil to the south. NST's half-hour time zone is unique to North America; only a few other places in the world, including central Australia and Sri Lanka, also operate on a half-hour time zone.

In 1963 the Newfoundland government attempted to put the entire province on Atlantic Time but much of the public protested and the government relented. Canadian time zone regulations enclose all of the province, including Labrador, within NST. As is the case in various other parts of the country, however, local time customs override federal concerns. Thus much of Labrador has chosen to follow Atlantic Standard Time.

before the *Mayflower* landed at Plymouth, Massachusetts, in 1620. Even so, St. John's has a somewhat limited number of buildings that pre-date 1800. The main building-destroyer has been fire. The 1892 fire, as well as others during the nineteenth century and even one that occurred in 1992, ravaged huge sections of the city. Each time St. John's has quickly rebuilt and the city is a charming mix of the modern and traditional. Residents and visitors enjoy various tree-studded parks, such as Victoria and C.A. Pippy. The latter's expansive grounds offer hiking trails, a golf course, the occasional moose sighting, and even a partially underground building that has windows into a living, trout-filled river.

■ *Modern buildings have begun to interrupt the traditional scene along St. John's waterfront.*

Hanging On in the Outports

Even after the abandonment of as many as three hundred small outports during the controversial resettlement drives of the 1950s and 1960s, Newfoundland still has upward of one thousand or so such communities. Many were founded as seasonal fishing camps. "When all the existing shore space became allocated," notes Jeff A. Webb, "or when more productive

■ *Much of downtown St. John's is a lively mix of shops and residences.*

fishing grounds became known, some people would move to other areas. These geographic and ecological factors account for the high number of small outports spread over the length of shoreline and hundreds of islands of Newfoundland and Labrador."[17]

Although outports differ from town to town and bay to bay, due to differences that can be traced to historical, religious, and economic reasons, they are typically small—or tiny. Many have a total population of fewer than five hundred residents. Because they started out as fishing villages, the houses, schools, stores, and churches are spread inland from the water's edge, where platforms for fish curing ("flakes") and wharves once acted as town squares. Although the Newfoundland government has built many new roads in recent years, some outports are still connected to neighboring towns mainly by ferries and other boat traffic.

Some outports like Petty Harbour on the outskirts of St. John's are successfully combining fishing with tourism, crafts, merchandizing, shipping, and industries such as paper milling. In those outports where fishing has not been replaced with more diversified economic options, especially the tiny outports located on islands in the various bays, the population is fast dwindling as old folk die and young people move away. For example, the population of the Great Northern Peninsula has shrunk by upward of 20 percent, down to about twenty thousand, in the decade since the cod moratorium in 1992. Those residents who are not leaving the outports for other provinces are mostly heading for the greater St. John's area—the Avalon peninsula now accounts for almost half of the province's total population.

Labrador: A Place Apart

Even though Labrador is not an island, like Newfoundland Island it is a sea-dominated place. Labrador has a mere forty miles (seventy kilometers) of paved highway in its entire Arizona-sized area. Most of this paved highway connects L'Anse-au-Clair on the Strait of Belle Isle to nearby Red Bay, though in 2002 the province completed a gravel, all-season highway from Red Bay to Cartwright. The Trans-Labrador Highway from Labrador City–Wabush to Happy Valley–Goose Bay has no services save in the Churchill Falls area. Meanwhile, the jagged coastline is some five thousand miles (eight thousand kilometers) long. Beyond Labrador City–Wabush, people travel mostly by boat or ferry, by plane, or by all-terrain-vehicles. During the winter, snowmobilers can take advantage of a newly completed trail system.

■ *Picturesque Petty Harbour is one of North America's oldest European-settled fishing villages.*

■ Traveling by Land and Sea

For a person who is afraid to fly, getting in and out of Newfoundland can be a time-consuming proposition. The two main ferry services from the south run from North Sydney, Nova Scotia, to Channel-Port aux Basques (year-round) and to Argentia in Placentia Bay (seasonal). The latter is a 325-mile (525-kilometer), thirteen-hour journey across the often rough seas of the Cabot Strait. The one-way fare for one person and a vehicle is about $200. Another long ferry ride awaits those who wish to travel from Lewisporte, in the island's Notre Dame Bay, to Labrador. The ferry stops in Cartwright before going on to Happy Valley-Goose Bay, and is also seasonal.

During the summer a ninety-minute ferry runs twice a day between St. Barbe on Newfoundland Island's west coast and Blanc Sablon on the Quebec-Labrador border. This ferry stops running, however, from early January through late April when the Strait of Belle Isle freezes over. Nor does this ferry deliver you to the "outside world." Highway 510 starts only a short distance south of Blanc Sablon, in Quebec. It winds its way north up the Labrador coast to Mary's Harbour and then cuts inland before returning to the coast at Cartwright, where it ends. But no roads from Canada's interior connect with 510 at Blanc Sablon, Cartwright, or anywhere else. Interprovincial seasonal ferries also bump up the coast of Labrador all the way to remote Nain.

For the truly determined it is possible to drive from, say, New York City to Happy Valley–Goose Bay. Figure about 18 hours for the 850 miles (1,350 kilometers) from New York to Baie Comeau on the north shore of the St. Lawrence River. Then it is on to the partially paved road that runs to Labrador City, just across the Quebec border, and the gravel Trans-Labrador Highway to Happy Valley–Goose Bay. Total anticipated travel time and distance: 36 hours to cover more than 1,500 miles (2,415 kilometers).

Labrador is very sparsely populated, having a mere 30,000 people out of the province's total population of 513,000. More than half of the people of Labrador, notes *National Geographic* writer Robert M. Poole, are congregated in four settlements:

> Labrador City and Wabush, adjoining towns carved out of the western wilderness in the 1950s and '60s, where iron-ore mining is the major business; Churchill Falls, a town founded in 1967 on the site of one of North America's large hydroelectric projects; and Happy Valley-Goose Bay, built during World War II as an airfield, now used by German, British, and Dutch fighter pilots for low-altitude training. Aside from a sprinkling of fishing settlements

along the coast, the rest of Labrador is lonely country, pa-
trolled by polar bears and wolves, foxes and caribou, black
bears and ptarmigan. And it is home to some of the
toughest and most resourceful humans you will find
anywhere.[18]

A half dozen or so tiny outpost towns survive on islands
and bays of the Labrador Sea north of Cartwright, with Nain
being the northernmost. These are mostly populated with native Innu and Inuit and accessed by air or seasonal boat service. The Labrador Sea coast also harbors dozens of seasonal
camps that do a thriving sportfishing business during the
brief summer. Sea ice forms along the Labrador coast during
the winter.

By far the two biggest metropolitan areas in Labrador are
a pair of twinned towns: Labrador City–Wabush and Happy
Valley–Goose Bay. Each area harbors about ten thousand people and is economically dependent upon a single industry.

Labrador City and Wabush, separated by only four miles
(seven kilometers), are situated on small lakes but have the
no-nonsense look of modern iron ore mining towns. The
population is younger than the provincial average, due to the
many young men drawn to the area to work in the iron ore
industry. The Iron Ore Company of Canada employs many
residents in its open-pit iron ore mine, the largest in Canada.
It and another mine in Wabush quarry and concentrate more
than half of Canada's iron ore. A railway hauls the product

■ *Archaeologists wash
dirt away from bits of
pottery at the excavations
of a whaling port in Red
Bay, Labrador.*

■ A Crisis of Spirit in Northern Labrador

Many Canadians were shocked in 1999 when a London-based human rights group compared the plight of Labrador's Innu to that of the Tibetans, the peaceful Asian people whose culture has been crushed by harsh Chinese rule since the late 1950s. In a widely read report, the group noted that one northern Labrador Innu town, Davis Inlet, appeared to have the highest annual suicide rate in the world.

Over the following year, as reporters investigated conditions in towns like Davis Inlet and Sheshatshiu, an Innu village of twelve hundred located near Happy Valley–Goose Bay, the news was even worse, if that is possible. In the popular Canadian weekly magazine *Maclean's*, writer John Demont described Sheshatshiu as "a nightmare of addiction, suicide, and violent death." He said that few people die of natural causes in the community since it is "estimated that well over half of adults are alcoholics, and domestic violence is widespread."

Print and television news reports prompted a public outcry and a promise of more social services from the provincial and federal governments. Dozens of teens were admitted to addiction treatment centers. Innu leaders say that the main problem is economic and cultural—the people have been uprooted from their traditional life. As recently as the late 1950s, many Innu still followed the caribou herds, their main source of food, clothing, and shelter. The Canadian government and the Catholic Church, however, encouraged the Innu to turn traditional summer settlements like Sheshatshiu into their permanent homes. Schools, churches, and medical facilities were built, but meaningful jobs were—and are—scarce.

In 2002 the Innu of Davis Inlet could finally embrace an alternative future: life in the newly built community of Natuashish. Located on the mainland a short distance from Davis Inlet, the new town cost the federal government, Newfoundland, and local Innu more than $100 million to construct and is complete with modern homes, a school, and a water treatment plant. Few Innu were reluctant to leave squalid Davis Inlet, with its overcrowded cabins and lack of plumbing, but Innu leaders realize that more comfortable living conditions is just one step. They hope to establish craft, ecotourism, and other enterprises to help rebuild the people's spirit.

south to Sept Isles, Quebec, for shipping to points in Canada, the United States, and Europe. Because world demand for iron ore fluctuates, however, Labrador City–Wabush has experienced recent periods of increased unemployment. City officials are hoping that the economy can diversify by developing new mining enterprises (companies have identified silica, graphite, and gold deposits), increasing tourism, promoting the hunting and fishing opportunities, and attracting geoscience and alternative energy research companies.

The highway connection that Labrador City–Wabush has with lower Canada, along with the proximity to hydroelectric power, allows the area to maintain the lowest cost of living in Labrador. Residents enjoy affordable housing, low electrical rates, year-round access to fresh produce, and a variety of retail stores that includes a number of national chains. Residents can even play an eighteen-hole golf course during the brief summer. The metro area is served by two public libraries, a daily newspaper, four schools plus a campus of the College of the North Atlantic, a fully accredited hospital, and a half dozen churches.

Labrador's other major metro area, Happy Valley–Goose Bay, sits at the western tip of Lake Melville, a long saltwater body that parallels the Mealy Mountains as it connects with the Labrador Sea. The area is a crossroads for road, sea, and air routes, making Happy Valley–Goose Bay a transportation hub for Labrador. It also remains an important training base for Canadian and European military pilots, although its airport is no longer the busiest in the world, as it once was during the height of the Cold War. The two towns developed as adjuncts to the training base, a place for employees and visitors to live and shop. The area has also attracted a diverse aboriginal population, including Innu, Inuit, and Métis. The economy has diversified somewhat in recent years to include shipping, adventure travel and tourism, and sport hunting (especially for caribou) and fishing. Happy Valley–Goose Bay is a service center for coastal towns on the Labrador Sea and for mining exploration and hydroelectric development in central and eastern Labrador. The town also promotes itself as "a modern, 'wired' community" whose high-speed Internet capabilities, Internet service providers, and web page designers make it "the recognized technological hub of Labrador."[19]

Ethnic Diversity in Newfoundland

During its period of most rapid expansion in the early nineteenth century, most of the new settlers to Newfoundland Island came from southwestern England and southeastern Ireland. After the 1840s, although many Irish fled Ireland due to the disastrous potato famine of 1848, relatively few came to Newfoundland, preferring Boston, New York, and other more southern ports. British immigration continued at a slow pace and the result is that the province today is overwhelmingly British and Irish in its ancestry. Some Highland Scots who settled part of the Codroy Valley on the southwestern coast in the mid-nineteenth century continue to lend that area a Scottish feel.

The descendents of French settlers now make up less than 5 percent of the population, although they are a vocal minority that works hard to keep their heritage respected in the province's schools, festivals, and culture. There are also remnants of the distinctive Portuguese and Basque communities that developed from the earliest fishing fleets. Some of the most recent immigrants include the Chinese. A pre-1949 policy prohibiting Chinese women from becoming Newfoundlanders kept their numbers down. Lebanese who were fleeing violence in their homeland also faced discrimination in Newfoundland but have managed to become respected citizens today. The island portion of the province has relatively few aboriginals, mainly some Mi'kmaq in a reserve and a few towns. Labrador has a higher concentration of First Nations.

In addition to Labrador's two thousand Innu (an additional fourteen thousand or so Innu live in communities in the Quebec section of the Ungava Peninsula), Labrador includes significant numbers of Inuit and Labrador Métis. The latter are the descendents of the fur traders and trappers who intermarried with native women starting in the early 1800s. Many Métis families stayed on in central Labrador to form small Métis communities. As part of the centralization movement of the 1950s and 1960s, the province successfully resettled some of these Métis in Goose Bay and other towns. The Métis have gained renewed respect as a distinct people in recent years, and in 1998 formed the roughly five-thousand-person Labrador Métis Nation. It has filed a comprehensive land claim with the Department of Indian Affairs and Northern Development in an effort to take control of lands the Métis have long occupied in central and southeastern Labrador.

■ *The Inuit of Labrador maintain a close connection to the land and the sea.*

■ A Distinctive Cuisine

Newfoundland's blend of English, Irish, French, and First Nations culture has resulted in a distinctive traditional cuisine. Of course the seafaring nature of the province means that fish figures prominently, with plenty of lobster, halibut, salmon, and trout, often prepared fresh using local ingredients. Cod is not as common as it once was but is still occasionally pan-fried fresh or used salted to make codfish au gratin, cod chowder, or brandade (pummeled cod mixed with potatoes). Corned beef and cabbage, sometimes referred to as Jigg's dinner, is often served at a traditional Newfoundland "scoff"—a hearty meal eaten as part of an impromptu party. Other popular traditional dishes include figgy duff, a steamed or boiled pudding with raisins; Newfoundland pea soup (with diced turnips); and blueberry upside-down cake. Newfoundlanders have also developed traditional game dishes. Those who are not ready to try "baked stuffed caribou heart" may be willing to try a moose burger.

A New Focus for Education

Until just recently, education in Newfoundland was dominated by religious forces. Newfoundland's earliest schools were organized in the 1700s by the Church of England and other religious groups. It was not until 1836 that the colonial government became directly involved by dispensing funds and establishing boards of education. Until joining Canada, Newfoundland's public school system lagged behind the Canadian average in standards and graduation rates, in part because funding was tied to fishery production rather than taxes.

As is the case in a number of other Canadian provinces, Newfoundland continues to partner with Roman Catholic, Presbyterian, and other religious groups and to fund church-administered education. Beginning in the early 1990s, however, Newfoundland government officials increasingly viewed education as the "key to economic development," according to Newfoundland and Labrador Heritage writer Phil McCann. "The new aim of education was to produce a flexible workforce with an entrepreneurial outlook suitable to the new global economy,"[20] he notes. As a result in 1997 the province passed a schools and education act that dramatically reduced the power and influence of the churches.

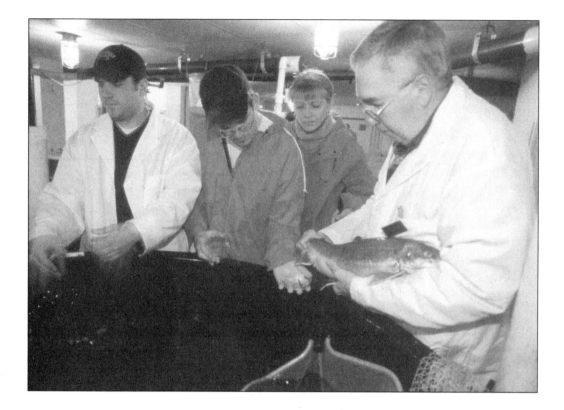

■ *Technicians at a Memorial University of Newfoundland marine station extract fish eggs.*

Newfoundland's new, mostly nondenominational school system is organized in ten regional districts plus a small (five-school) provincial-wide Francophone (French-speaking) district. The largest of the districts is Avalon East, which includes St. John's. Its sixty-seven schools have some thirty thousand pupils and two thousand teachers. Overall the province has nearly five hundred schools (including seven private schools) covering kindergarten to grade twelve, with six thousand teachers and ninety thousand students. French immersion programs are offered in forty-nine schools.

Newfoundland's only university, Memorial University of Newfoundland, was founded in 1925 in St. John's. In 1975 a local campus in Corner Brook was opened as Sir Wilfred Grenfell College, named after the early twentieth-century medical missionary. Memorial University of Newfoundland is also one of two Canadian universities with a British campus, in Harlow. Memorial has more than thirteen thousand full-time students taking courses in everything from visual arts to fisheries resource management. The university is well known for its strong teaching and research departments. Newfoundland also has three campuses of the public College of the North Atlantic; three government-funded postsecondary institutes specializing in applied arts and technology and fisheries and marine technology; five regional community colleges; and more than three dozen private training institutions.

A Strong Commitment to Health Care

Newfoundland has a smaller private health sector than most other provinces but an active and committed public sector, supported by provincial funding that has increased in recent years at a faster rate than the national average. In fact, health care now claims more than forty cents of every government dollar spent in the province, with the cost per resident for providing health care above $2,000 per year (about $80 above the Canadian average). Rapid increases in the costs of drugs, hospitalization, and physician services are pinching expenditures, but the province—unlike Alberta, for example—remains committed to the public health model.

"Our total public and private expenditures on health care in Newfoundland and Labrador have increased every year except one from 1975 to 1999," according to Joan Marie Aylward, minister of Health and Community Services. "From 1995 to 1999, our total health dollars per capita has grown by

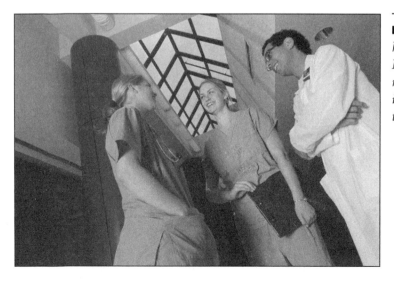

■ *Doctors and other health care workers in Newfoundland are committed to extending quality services throughout the province.*

18 percent versus the national average of 11 percent, and our public sector expenditures per capita has grown by 19 percent versus the 8 percent national average."[21]

The public funds are necessary to combat a number of challenging health care issues. The siting of the many outports in remote coves, with often difficult travel connections, can mean that access to high-quality health care is limited for many rural residents. Newfoundland has also experienced difficulties attracting and keeping doctors, nurses, and other professionals. As a result the province tends to score near the bottom of the Canadian average in measures such as infant mortality, life expectancy, and heart disease.

Sports and Recreation in Newfoundland

Many Newfoundland residents take advantage of the area's reliable ice and snow by embracing various winter sports. Marble Mountain just outside of Corner Brook offers prime downhill skiing, not so much for its relatively tame vertical drop but for its astounding annual snowfall—its sixteen feet (five meters) of snow in an average year is more than anywhere else in eastern North America. The frequent fresh powder also means plenty of opportunities for cross-country skiers and wilderness snowmobilers, often through April on the island and even later into the

■ *Nature is a generous snowmaker for skiers in the Corner Brook area.*

■ An Unusual Tourist Attraction: Iceberg Watching

Many people come to St. John's and other parts of Newfoundland just to experience the wonder of seeing a 150-foot- (50-meter) high, 100-million-ton iceberg slowly float into view. Passing icebergs are a regular summer pleasure in the "iceberg alley" off Newfoundland's northeast coast. These icebergs with their ten-thousand-year-old ice have been calved from Greenland's western glaciers. The Labrador Current carries the massive chunks of frozen fresh water past Newfoundland on their way south and east.

North Twillingate Island in Notre Dame Bay is one of the best places in the world to see icebergs. Starting in the late spring, they can be viewed from shore, from one of the boat tours, or, for the adventuresome, from a sea kayak. Viewers are warned not to get too close. Icebergs are melting as they slowly drift southward, and they can calve, turn, and otherwise evolve in ways that can be dangerous to observe from close up. Of the ten thousand or so bergs that are liberated each year from Greenland glaciers, perhaps two thousand make it as far as Newfoundland over the course of a year or two. Even fewer make it out into the Gulf Stream, where they can pose a hazard to ships. It was one such iceberg that sank the *Titanic* in the North Atlantic about 400 miles (650 kilometers) from Newfoundland on April 15, 1912.

The iceberg tours often also provide the opportunity to see a score of sea mammal species that arrive every spring to feed in the rich waters, including harbor porpoises, saddleback dolphins, and minke, fin, sperm, and other whales. Each year an estimated five thousand humpback whales cruise into the coastal waters of Newfoundland, where they can be seen breaching their forty-ton bodies out of the water in dramatic leaps.

■ *Majestic icebergs thrill tourists.*

spring in much of Labrador. The Labrador City–Wabush area has hundreds of miles of groomed snowmobile trails. Island ski tour companies offer fresh-powder enthusiasts the opportunity to travel to remote areas on heated, ten-person snowcats.

Gros Morne and other places are also world-class sites for ice climbing. "What makes climbing ice in Newfoundland so unique," notes a climbing website, "is that many of the climbs rely more on water seeping over cliffs next to the ocean and are not fed by large waterfalls. Not only does this provide for spectacular scenery it also makes it easy to approach."[22]

Summer sports run the gamut from soccer and tennis to hiking and boating. Because of its spectacular coastal scenery, Newfoundland is becoming a destination site for sea kayaking.

The provincial population is too low to support top-level professional football or hockey teams, as there are in most other provinces. Since 1991, however, St. John's has been the home of the American Hockey League Maple Leafs, a minor-league affiliate of the Toronto Maple Leafs of the National Hockey League. The St. John's Maple Leafs play an eighty-game schedule against rivals such as the Saint John (New Brunswick) Flames and the Hamilton (Ontario) Bulldogs. In October 2001 the Maple Leafs played their first game in the new Mile One Stadium in front of a franchise record crowd of more than six thousand fans.

A Connection to the Past

Many of the people of Newfoundland live with a vital sense of connection to the past. This pride in heritage is expressed in a number of ways, from the area's distinctive words and language to the preservation of wharves and public buildings. It is also apparent in Newfoundland's unique arts and culture.

Arts and Culture

chapter 5

D ue to Newfoundland's location and heritage, the province's seafaring history has had a major influence on the arts and culture, from maritime museums to popular regattas. Newfoundland has also long been a place where various cultures have shaped one another, including First Nations, English, French, Portuguese, and more. The result is a lively mix of the traditional and the modern. The provincial government has long encouraged this cultural stew by offering official support for the arts. These efforts continue to this day in the organization and funding of folk festivals, craft societies, a home-grown film industry, and more. It even organizes "cultural trade missions" to other cities. As *Boston Globe* correspondent Leslie Brokaw noted, "What's not to love about a government that puts the same energies into promoting its cultural exports as it does its other homegrown businesses?"[23]

Celebrating a Maritime Heritage

Newfoundland's marine environment is a major source of artistic and cultural inspiration for the province's many distinctive museums, centers, and galleries. This is particularly evident in Newfoundland's most ambitious new heritage center, "The Rooms," a state-of-the-art $50 million project being built in St. John's. It will provide a home for three prominent cultural institutions now housed separately: the Provincial Museum of Newfoundland and Labrador, the Provincial Archives of Newfoundland and Labrador, and the Art Gallery of Newfoundland and Labrador. Moreover, a government website notes, "The work of visual artists has concentrated heavily on the majestic scenery of Newfoundland and

Labrador and on the depiction of objects, ranging from fish and marine animals to fishing gear and rustic houses, which are part of everyday life."[24]

Other museums, festivals, and cultural centers in the province also reflect a maritime heritage. For example, the Sparkes Heritage House Lifestyle Museum in Sibley's Cove, on Trinity Bay, has costumed interpreters demonstrating a 1930s fishing family's lifestyle. South of Harbour Grace, the Hibbs Cove Fishing Museum offers visitors the chance to walk amidst a traditional fish flake, fisherman's home, and schoolhouse. Visitors to the *Mathew* in Bonavista can tour the decks of a replica of the ship John Cabot sailed from England in 1497. Approximately half a million people visit the province's many community or provincially operated museums and heritage sites.

Fishy Festivals and Fun Events

Many of the annual celebrations that occur around the province are distinctive to the people and the locale. With Newfoundland's long and snowy winter, the province is an ideal place for various winter attractions. St. John's, Corner Brook, and numerous towns and outports hold well-attended

---

■ Reinventing "The Rooms"

The Rooms is being constructed on the side of a hill where Fort Townshend once overlooked the city and the harbor. Because the fort ruins have yielded a treasure trove of archaeological artifacts, The Rooms will be one of the only facilities in North America to incorporate an active archaeological excavation within its walls. The Rooms, notes the center's website, will "restore the site to its former prominence as a social and cultural centre in this city. By enclosing parts of the Fort Townshend ruins *within* the new building, we can make use of interactive displays, audio-visual and printed materials as well as other technologies which don't work outdoors."

The name "The Rooms" comes from local custom. Newfoundland fishermen called a fishing room the land, with its buildings, flakes, and wharves, where they would bring their catch for curing and related activities. The Rooms will hold provincial artifacts ranging from items recovered from the *Titanic* to a traditional kitchen coal bucket. The heritage center will also house archival material and diverse works of art. City officials expect to open The Rooms in 2004.

winter carnivals that feature ice sculptures, parades, and games. Winter competitions include the annual Grenfell Snowmobile Ride, a 125-mile (200-kilometer) race from St. Anthony to Main Brook, and sled dog races in the Labrador towns of Wabush, Hopedale, and Port Hope Simpson.

It is during the summer, however, that the province comes alive with festivals and events. Residents and visitors can choose from folk festivals and Canada Day celebrations in numerous cities; theater festivals in Gros Morne, Carbonear, and elsewhere; and craft fairs in diverse locations. Many coastal towns and villages celebrate offerings of the sea by holding festivals devoted to crabs, lobsters, shrimp, and other fish. Newfoundland also has its strawberry and blueberry festivals. Towns on the French Shore are famous for their celebrations of French music, culture, and cuisine. Even British-founded St. John's holds a three-day Franco-Fest. St. John's cultural schedule features Shakespeare by the Sea, an international choral event known as Sharing the Voices, and the wildly popular annual regatta (rowing race).

■ *A drama about a nurse known as the "Florence Nightingale of the North" was a hit at the Gros Morne Theatre Festival.*

A popular summer activity is to explore one of the many "loop drives" along Newfoundland's coast. For example, along the so-called Irish loop, going south from St. John's through Ferryland, Trepassey, and St. Mary's, people can enjoy not only the rolling green hills but also Irish-influence festivals. One of the best is the Southern Shore Shamrock Festival, held in Ferryland in July. Farther to the southwest is the "French Ancestor's Route," also called the Festival Coast for the many French-flavored festivals.

A Thriving Crafts Industry

Some two thousand provincial residents are employed in the crafts industry, creating works with a production value approaching $40 million annually. Contemporary artists work in a range of media, including wood, metal, glass, clay, and textiles, often incorporating themes and images of ships, the sea, harbors, icebergs, and dories. "The earliest crafts—boatbuilding, net-knitting, and the making of items such as jiggers [unbaited, weighted hooks], killicks [simple, homemade anchors for nets], and all the curious implements of a fisherman's livelihood—were survival crafts," notes writer and needlework designer Catherine Simpson. "Although many of the old survival crafts are now in decline," she says, "some have taken on new life as contemporary craftspeople adapt old traditions for new markets and country decor."[25] Patterned knitwork inspired by netmaking techniques and miniature wooden boxes inspired by roughhewn kitchen breadboxes are just two examples of crafts that meld the traditional and the modern.

■ A Royal Regatta

St. John's is the site of North America's oldest continuous sporting event, the Royal St. John's Regatta. The first organized regatta was held in 1818 and except for a few years when wars or other disasters intervened it has been held annually since then. It is a major event for the city and the island, weather-permitting now held on the first Wednesday in August and officially a municipal and provincial holiday in metropolitan St. John's. The regatta is held on Quidi Vidi Lake, a short stroll from the harbor. Crews row six-member, fixed-seat racing shells that are as identical as possible over a 2.45 kilometer (men) or 1.225 kilometer (women) course (this translates to 1.5 and 0.75 miles). The regatta attracts up to forty thousand spectators who come not only for the exciting races but the festival-like atmosphere, complete with booths and concessions, that line the shores.

■ *Boats have been racing at the Royal St. John's Regatta for almost two centuries.*

Native peoples of Labrador are well represented in the industry, and Simpson notes that their traditional art forms are quite distinct from the mostly European-derived artistic traditions of Newfoundland Island. For example, Innu artisans make popular handsewn tea dolls, which were originally fashioned by migratory Innu bands to allow children to carry a needed supply. Each of the traditionally dressed cloth dolls are stuffed with about two pounds (one kilogram) of loose tea. Inuit soapstone sculptors and grasswork bowlmakers are also increasingly finding an appreciative audience locally and beyond.

■ *Tea dolls are outfitted with the traditional garb of Labrador Innu.*

The crafts industry enjoys considerable government support. The province has developed a "Crafts of Character" program that promotes local products at trade shows, nationally and internationally, and supports craft sales and exports. "Through various programs," Simpson says, "the provincial government has encouraged the development of crafts as an economically important cultural industry. Craftspeople from all over the world have chosen to make their homes here, grafting fresh ideas and professional experience onto the perennial rootstock of traditional craft and stimulating cross-fertilization of old and new."[26]

A Literary Tradition

One book in particular—E. Annie Proulx's Pulitzer Prize–winning 1993 novel *The Shipping News*, memorably set in Newfoundland—has put Newfoundland on the literary map. It has also put Newfoundland on the literal map: In 2002 the provincial tourism board estimated the value of Canadian editorial coverage to date for *The Shipping News* alone at over $1 million, enhancing awareness of the province as a destination. Proulx's account of a Brooklyn-born man who returns to his ancestral home—"the old place of the Quoyles, half ruined, isolated, the walls and doors of it pumiced by stony lives of dead generations"[27]—in Newfoundland offers penetrating insights into island customs and places.

A number of other literary works in the past and present have solidified the province's reputation as a fertile source of

■ *Novelist E. Annie Proulx, shown here in Vermont in 1994, drew upon her experience living in Newfoundland to write the prize-winning* The Shipping News.

material and inspiration for writers. For example, local writer Bernice Morgan has rivaled Proulx for popular if not critical success. Her novels about the struggle of early settlers, including *Random Passage* and *Waiting for Time*, have gained readers locally and nationally. *Random Passage*, which explores outport life during the nineteenth century, was made into a mini-series TV movie that aired in early 2002.

Novelists like Proulx and Morgan can draw upon Newfoundland's rich folk literature. This traditional literature, notes a government website,

> dependent on the spoken rather than the written word and circulated by word of mouth and customary practice—developed and flourished alongside the more familiar forms of written expression. Among the genres of oral literature to be found in the Newfoundland context are folksongs and ballads, folk drama, proverbs, rhymes, riddles, jokes, recitations and monologues, local legends, personal experience narratives, and folktales.[28]

Newfoundland's folk literature is so rich it has inspired the province to publish its own five-thousand-word dictionary.

Film and Video Take Off

Newfoundland's scenic potential has long drawn filmmakers in search of the right material for documentaries and nature films. Newfoundland Island was a location for such Hollywood feature films as *The Viking* (1931) and *Orca the Killer Whale* (1977) as well as numerous documentaries, shorts, and independent films since then. The first feature film both filmed and produced in Newfoundland was the quirky comedy *The Adventures of Faustus Bidgood,* about a low-level bureaucrat who becomes the post-revolution leader of the People's Republic of Newfoundland. *Bidgood* was a low-budget production that took ten years to fund and shoot before being released, to modest commercial success, in 1986.

In the years since that breakthrough, Newfoundland's film and video industry has expanded to include scores of feature films and television shows conceived and filmed in Newfoundland, with recent years producing a peak of activity. Perhaps the most prominent recent project was the filming in 2000 of the eight-part television series *Random Passage.* Officials say that the province's film and video industry is now a $20 million per year enterprise, based almost entirely in St. John's. The St. John's International Women's Film and Video Festival, held mid-October, shines a spotlight on some of the best work from independent filmmakers. The Newfoundland and Labrador Film Development Corporation provides public funding and tax incentives to expand the provincial film industry. Just as influential is the Newfoundland Independent Filmmaker's Cooperative, a widely respected, member-based trade group that provides filmmakers with training, equipment, sound studios, and other crucial resources.

■ Arts and Crafts Go Online

Newfoundland has recently pioneered online sales of its residents' arts and crafts products. In 2001, the member-based Craft Council of Newfoundland and Labrador (CCNL) became the first craft industry association in Canada to launch an online store (www.craftcouncil.nf.ca). The CCNL Online Store features hundreds of items with full-color photos and descriptive text. Prices range from less than $15 for holiday ornaments, glass suncatchers, and handpainted wooden earrings to more than $5,000 for a quilt made by St. John's artist Jack Eastwood. Consumers have purchased pottery, blown glass, jewelry, craft kits, and other products from around the corner and around the world.

The CCNL's Devon House Craft Centre operates out of a historic stone and brick building in downtown St. John's. The Craft Centre serves as the council's administrative headquarters and houses a library and resource center. It also contains an extensive craft gallery, a gift shop, and studio spaces for teaching and making pottery and other crafts.

■ *Traditional folk artists like 1950s fiddler Tom Jennings helped to keep alive Newfoundland's connections to its rich past.*

From Mummering to the Blues

The visual and performing arts have undergone something of a revival in the past twenty years as artists have increasingly expressed a distinct Newfoundland perspective imbued with an independent spirit. Folk performance arts have long been strong, such as storytelling, traditional dance, and fiddle playing. Lately these traditional art forms have been imbued with a new energy, noted St. John's novelist Michael Crummey upon returning to his native province after a thirteen-year spell in Ontario:

> What I've found most striking since returning is the now of what's happening here, the spark and range of the new. Original live theatre and readings, festivals of new dance, of independent film. A mass youth choir of singers from Newfoundland and 14 countries at this year's Festival 500 opening their performance with an Estonian folk song and closing with a new arrangement of Feller from Fortune. Seventy-two-year-old blues journeyman Eddie Kirkland from Macon, Ga., playing an unrehearsed show with three young St. John's musicians at a downtown bar, the local guys craning to catch Kirkland's chord changes as they went, the crowd keeping them onstage until 3:30 in the morning.[29]

The strange local tradition of mummering, handed down from the Romans to the British, might also be included as a folk art. Mummers traditionally wandered into the homes of wealthy people during the holiday season to perform short

■ The Shepherds Share Artistic Success

Helen Parsons Shepherd and Reginald Shepherd, a pair of native-born New-foundlanders who have been married for more than fifty years, are among the most prominent painters in Newfoundland. Helen was raised in an artis-tically inclined St. John's family—her father was a poet and her brother Paul Parsons also developed into a noted artist. In 1948 she was the first New-foundlander to obtain an art degree at the Ontario College of Art. It was there that Helen met fellow student Reginald Shepherd, an aspiring young artist who had been born in Conception Bay. Reginald had been inspired to pursue art fulltime while a soldier stationed at Gander during World War II.

The couple married in 1948 and moved to St. John's, where they reno-vated a downtown house to include art studios as well as space for an art school. The Newfoundland Academy of Art, which they founded, was New-foundland's first art school. For the next dozen years they taught and influ-enced a generation of young artists who flocked to the school. After closing the school in the early 1960s to devote themselves entirely to painting, Helen and Reginald gained national prominence for their work. Helen's formal por-traits, including a number of prominent Newfound-land figures, and her color-ful still lifes, are widely admired. Reginald's land-scapes and street scenes, painted in a style he has described as "poetic real-ism," often are inspired by his childhood experiences in Conception Bay.

The Shepherds are re-tirement age but remain ac-tive artists, spending their winters in St. John's and summers in Clarke's Beach painting and sketching.

■ Farmers Market, Churchill Sq., *oil by Helen Parsons Shepherd.*

plays, hoping for a donation. A peculiar rural Newfoundland variant is for mummers to disguise themselves and enter friends' homes to play tricks, or just drink the hosts' alcohol, until they can guess who they are. Complementing such tra-ditions in Newfoundland today is a diverse range of profes-sional theatrical companies, choirs, and musical groups.

The provincial government has undertaken a number of innovative programs such as "cultural trade missions" to other cities to help support the arts. For example, in the fall of 2001 provincial arts officials escorted twenty-four musicians, visual artists, and filmmakers to Boston to meet with New England–based management companies, gallery curators, and radio stations. "A government agency picked a regional industry with export potential," reported Leslie Brokaw, "targeted a specific foreign country, invited participants to apply to attend, and then coordinated the several-day trip. Artists paid some of the costs, but the government is paying the bulk of the tab with the idea that the efforts will be an economic plus in the long term."[30] Government officials said that the week-long trip, which was Newfoundland's ninth cultural trade mission to New England in the past few years, provided an opportunity to show off some of the province's strongest artists, including the folk/pop group Rasa, the Celtic-flavored rock group The Punters, pop band Timber, and visual artist Christine Koch.

Culture and Economy

The people of the province have an abundance of opportunities to enrich body and soul, but factors such as Newfoundland's geographic isolation and its difficulties in developing a diversified economy mean that it will face challenging issues in the near future.

Current Challenges

CHAPTER

6

Newfoundland has changed rapidly in the past decade as the traditional reliance on fishing and mining has given way to new industries, including oil and hydroelectric, that nevertheless pose a familiar challenge: how to balance the potential conflicts between economic security, environmental harmony, and social cohesion. Drilling for offshore oil and the building of massive hydroelectric plants in Labrador offer economic promise as well as potential environmental peril. The government has been pursuing new mines, especially in Labrador, and new lumbering operations—forests and paper mills in the Corner Brook area and elsewhere now supply a significant chunk of Canada's newsprint—but environmentalists and local residents are wary of adverse effects. The Newfoundland government is also increasingly finding it difficult to tax and regulate these industries because companies threaten to leave—and take jobs with them—when faced with government restrictions.

Is Cod Dead?

It has been more than a decade since the disastrous collapse of Newfoundland's cod fishery. Canadian officials initially predicted the fishery would be reopened by the year 2000. As of early 2003, the cod have not returned. The province is now forced to confront the possibility that the Grand Banks cod fishery suffered not merely a severe blow but a fatal wound in the early 1990s.

Exactly why the cod fishery has been so slow to recover is somewhat of a mystery, since cod populations have been known to recover in other areas. As Mark Kurlansky points out:

> Fueling optimism is the fact that decimated cod stocks have been restored fairly quickly in other countries. In 1989, the Norwegian government realized its cod stocks were in a serious decline. It severely restricted the fishery, putting many fishermen, fish-plant workers, and boat builders out of business and drastically reducing the size of its fleet. . . . But because the government instituted these measures while the stock was still commercially viable, while there were still some large spawners left, the cod population stabilized and started increasing after a few years.[31]

Whether the Grand Banks fishery will follow this Norwegian scenario is unknown. It is possible that enough large and still-fertile cod survived the massive over-fishing and the population will slowly recover. Cod ecology is complex and the recovery rate may be affected by various factors, including climatic changes, water temperature, and other species (like arctic cod, usually considered a noncommercial fish) that move into its range and prevent its reestablishment.

The silver lining to Newfoundland's ongoing cod crisis is that the province has managed to develop a more diversified fishery in the past decade. The crab and shrimp caught and processed in Newfoundland now account for about 75 percent of the value of the fishing industry. In fact, the province is now the world's largest producer of cold-water cooked and peeled shrimp. At fifteen thousand workers, overall employment in the fishing industry is still down from pre-1992 highs but represents a significant contribution to the overall economy. Newfoundland has also made giant strides in developing a thriving aquaculture industry that cultivates Atlantic salmon, steelhead trout, cod, and other fish. The provincial government's generous funding of the fishing industry has been a major factor in turning around this segment of the economy.

Liquid Gold: Newfoundland's New Energy Industry

Fortunately for Newfoundland, the collapse of the cod fishery in 1992 coincided closely with the birth of a suddenly thriving commercial energy industry. Oil reserves have been known to exist on Newfoundland Island since 1867, when an

exploratory well in Parson's Pond, on the west coast of the Northern Peninsula, hit oil. A small refinery there in the first decade of the twentieth century was Newfoundland's earliest commercial oil production but the industry remained a provincial afterthought until the 1960s. That is when researchers identified offshore Newfoundland, and to a lesser degree offshore Labrador, as prime territory for locating petroleum reserves.

Hundreds of exploratory wells drilled in the years since have confirmed that the Jeanne d'Arc Basin, in the area of the Grand Banks, is the site of a number of major oil fields. The largest strikes in the basin were made at Hibernia in 1979, Hebron–Ben Nevis in 1981, and Terra Nova and White Rose in 1984. The total recoverable resource in the basin may be as high as 2 billion barrels of oil—enough to cover Canada's total annual oil consumption for three years—plus 5 trillion cubic feet of natural gas. There have also been a half dozen significant strikes of natural gas in the Labrador Sea.

It takes years to construct the massive offshore oil rigs necessary to extract oil from beneath the ocean floor so

■ Onsite at Hibernia

About 210 miles (315 kilometers) east of St. John's, anchored in 260 feet (80 meters) of the dark and cold waters of the North Atlantic, is one of the world's largest offshore oil drilling rigs. Overall the Hibernia rig weighs more than 1 million tons and is taller than a seventy-story building. It is massive enough to provide living and working quarters for some two hundred workers, from drillers to cooks, at a time. Its topside bristles with elaborate oil technology capable of pumping more than 180,000 barrels a day from the 3-billion-barrel oil field beneath the ocean's floor (of which perhaps one-third is recoverable).

Hibernia was made massive to increase both its productivity and its safety—Newfoundlanders have not forgotten a disaster that happened in February 1982 at Hibernia. A winter storm capsized and sank the Ocean Ranger, a floating exploratory drilling platform, leaving its entire eighty-four-man crew dead in the water. Hibernia was designed to withstand severe storms as well as a potential direct hit from a 6-million-ton iceberg (which can be expected to occur about every ten thousand years).

One key to Hibernia's stability is its two-piece construction. A special 345-foot- (105-meter) high, 450,000-ton gravity-base structure (GBS) was built at the Bull Arm Fabrication and Construction Site in Trinity Bay, Newfoundland. The GBS was floated to the offshore site and partially submerged. An equal weight of solid ballast was added to secure it in place on the ocean floor. The GBS has storage tanks for more than 1 million barrels of crude oil, plus shafts for the drills that reach down to the ocean floor. The 37,000-ton topsides facility was transported by barges to the site and attached to the GBS. Various huge modules are used for drilling and processing the oil as well as for staff accommodations, a helideck, and lifeboat stations.

Hibernia did not start producing oil until late 1997 and Terra Nova until early 2002. The two fields combined to produce upward of 100 million barrels of oil in 2002, with a production value in excess of $3 billion, making offshore oil Newfoundland's highest valued commodity. The White Rose field may be in production by 2004. Even the onshore oil industry is ramping up in the province: A number of exploratory wells in western Newfoundland have shown promise, and the Garden Hill oil and gas field at Port au Port commenced production in mid-2002. Newfoundland is now Canada's second-leading oil producer, after Alberta.

As potentially lucrative as the oil industry is, concerns exist that the province is not reaping its fair share of the benefits. The oil rigs, an oil refinery recently opened in Placentia Bay, the massive Bull Arm construction site, and shipment facilities have not yielded huge numbers of new jobs. The Canadian and Newfoundland governments also had to pour about $1.5 billion into building the Hibernia rig, through grants, tax exemptions, and loans. (The rest of the $6 billion tag was picked up by a consortium of six companies, including Mobil Oil Canada, Chevron Canada Resources, and Petro-Canada.) Some of this government money is coming back to the public in the form of royalties the consortium pays for extracting the oil. Economists disagree as to whether the royalties from Hibernia will ever equal the amount of government money put into the project. If it ends up being a money loser, it will not be Newfoundland's first industrial endeavor to fail to meet high expectations.

A Bum Deal Haunts Newfoundland

When Newfoundland premier Joey Smallwood signed a pact with Quebec in 1969 to share the revenue from a new hydro-electric power project in Labrador, no one knew that this would come to be known as one of the most spectacularly one-sided deals in Canadian history. Newfoundland suffers to this day from the deal's lopsided terms, which have reaped billions of dollars for Quebec but relatively little for Newfoundland.

The agreement committed Newfoundland to selling most of the electricity to Quebec for less than one cent per kilowatt hour until 2041. As the average price of electricity has risen to more than five cents per kilowatt hour for industrial users, and double that for consumers, Quebec has been in the enviable position of selling electricity for a fraction of what it paid Newfoundland. Quebec's windfall profits of more than $600 million per year from Churchill Falls means that over the life of the contract it would receive some 96 percent of the project's profits.

The most obvious problem with the contract, from Newfoundland's point of view, is that it commits the province to selling the Churchill Falls electricity for sixty-five years at 1960s prices. Because the retail price of electricity has increased substantially over the past four decades, this is an incredible windfall for Quebec at Newfoundland's expense.

Newfoundland leaders tried without success for many years to reopen the contract with Hydro-Quebec. Quebec has never really been happy about how Canada gave Labrador to Newfoundland in 1929, since it considered the entire Ungava Peninsula to be part of Quebec. So it refused to alter the deal in Newfoundland's favor. In the 1980s Newfoundland finally filed a lawsuit that went to Canada's Supreme Court. Unfortunately for Newfoundland, the court refused to order that the contract be renegotiated. The impasse became so angry that at one point Newfoundland threatened to shut down the

■ Churchill Falls Part Two

For much of the past decade the government of Newfoundland has been enmeshed in negotiations with the Innu and Hydro-Quebec, Quebec's publicly owned power company, about plans for a new hydroelectric complex in central Labrador. Dubbed Lower Churchill because it would be sited on the Lower Churchill River about 125 miles (200 kilometers) south of the existing Churchill Falls project, the proposal is potentially the second largest hydroelectric construction project in the world (after China's Three Gorges Dam). It would cost as much as $13 billion and take years to divert two rivers from Quebec into a catchment area. Other aspects to the project include building two dams, constructing new transmission lines, and upgrading the existing facility at Churchill Falls.

In 2002 the Newfoundland government was claiming to be close to a final deal on the project. Premier Roger Grimes's government clearly was eager to get the project underway, noting that electricity from the new plant could provide power for communities locally and on Newfoundland Island. The government was also planning on using Lower Churchill to power future industrial projects, including a nickel refining plant on the island, and to gain additional public revenue from sales to Hydro-Quebec.

Just as the project seemed finally to get on track, however, more snags appeared, mainly relating to the question of whether Newfoundland would benefit enough from the project. Politicians in the opposition Conservative Party said that Newfoundland should not be rushed into concluding a deal. "While few details of the proposed deal have emerged," according to business reporter Kevin Cox, "there is growing anger in Newfoundland and Labrador that Quebec, which is proposing to finance construction of the plant, will gain the lion's share of benefits from the project as it does from the Upper Churchill development." In late 2002 two members of the board of Newfoundland and Labrador Hydro resigned in protest over the deal. Innu opposition also remains vocal, suggesting that Lower Churchill is hardly a done deal.

■ *A spillway at Churchill Falls is part of the vast hydroelectric complex.*

power station at Churchill Falls and let it sit idle until the contract expired in 2041.

Quebec finally relented in 2000 and agreed to revise some parts of the deal, at least in part because it was clear that the Churchill Falls deal was a major stumbling block to progress on Lower Churchill Falls. The revised deal should allow Newfoundland to potentially show a gain of more than $2 billion by the end of the contract in 2041 rather than the loss projected by the terms of the original contract.

Political Hardball at Voisey's Bay

Newfoundland's leaders in recent years have been very wary of repeating the mistake made in the hydroelectric deal with Quebec, both in the realm of power generation and resource exploitation. A major concern has been that mining companies would extract valuable resources from the province but then ship the raw ore elsewhere for processing. When that happens the province gains some mining jobs and royalty income but is denied the much more substantial economic benefits from the operation of processing facilities. In 1995 Newfoundland passed a law that established serious financial penalties for any mining company that shipped unrefined mineral ore from the province.

The most prominent test case for this new resource policy quickly became what has been identified as the world's largest nickel ore deposit at Voisey's Bay, on the northern Labrador coast. A pair of St. John's prospectors identified the deposit in 1993 and set off a corporate rush to stake out claims. The deposit has since been valued at more than $50 billion because of its high nickel (as well as copper and cobalt) content and because it is located on the edge of the Labrador Sea, allowing for relatively cheap shipment. During the mid-1990s Toronto-based International Nickel Company (Inco) outbid other mining companies to take a controlling interest in the project. Its exploratory drilling generated an immediate protest from native groups and led to long negotiations with the provincial government.

Because the Voisey's Bay site is sandwiched between the Inuit town of Nain to the north and the Innu towns of Davis Inlet and Natuashish to the south, both of these native groups have long claimed ownership of Voisey's Bay, referred to as Emish by the Innu and Tasiujatsoak by the Inuit. Inco initially took little heed of their land claims, leading the native groups to a rare instance of active collaboration on a political goal. Some of the subsequent native protests were dramatic—in 1995 a militant group of Innu attacked a drilling site, burning a pumphouse and smashing equipment. Newfoundland sent in the Royal Canadian Mounted Police to allow the exploratory operations to continue.

Refine It or Leave It

Newfoundland government officials were more concerned with jobs than native rights. They insisted that any nickel mined in the province also had to be processed at a refinery in the province. "If we don't get the smelter, Inco doesn't get the mine,"[32] government negotiator Bill Rowat proclaimed in 1998. Inco balked, saying that the price of nickel was too low and that it would rather process the nickel outside the province than invest in building a smelter in Newfoundland. Negotiations involving the government of Newfoundland, the Innu Nation, the Labrador Inuit Association, and Inco dragged on for years.

Finally in June 2002 the four parties reached an agreement on the principal issues to develop Voisey's Bay. The mining company agreed to construct a concentrating plant at Voisey's Bay. Inco also committed to building a nickel processing facility and warehouse at Argentia on Newfoundland Island, though not necessarily before the first ore shipments would begin to leave the open pit mines at Voisey's Bay. Finally, Inco agreed to

establish a research center at the St. John's campus of Memorial University of Newfoundland. Government officials said that although the deal was not perfect—Inco held out for significant tax breaks—it was possible that, perhaps ten years down the line when underground mining, the processing facility, and the research center are fully operational, a total of 1,250 jobs would be created. Newfoundland education minister Judy Foote proclaimed Voisey's Bay "a very significant deal for our Province that I think will go down in history as one of the best deals that this Province has ever seen."[33]

Innu and Inuit leaders were also happy with the deal. Newfoundland agreed to share mine-generated royalty revenues. Inco agreed to train natives for jobs in all phases of the project and to hire aboriginal groups for construction and spin-off work. The native groups will also remain involved in the ongoing regulatory and project development efforts.

The Bowater pulp and paper mill, shown here circa 1950, is one of the firms that led Corner Brook to be dubbed "the city that paper built."

Turning Around "the Appalachia of Canada"

Initiatives such as Hibernia, Terra Nova, and Voisey's Bay, as well as new fishing and lumbering operations, have been crucial in slowly changing the perception of Newfoundland as "the Appalachia of Canada." Newfoundland's reputation as the poorest province in Canada has long been based on its sky-high unemployment rate. Even with the recent oil development and advances in manufacturing, the unemployment rate remained above 16 percent in 2001. Although this was the lowest rate in Newfoundland since 1989, it was the highest rate in Canada and stratospheric by the standards of most Western democracies.

The long-term effects of high unemployment can be disastrous for an area. The government must pay enormous sums of money into welfare and unemployment programs, yet the

■ Last Person Leaving: Turn Off the Lights

Most of Newfoundland is sparsely populated—and becoming increasingly so. During the decade of the 1990s the province's net out-migration—the number of residents leaving the province to live elsewhere minus newcomers—amounted to almost fifty thousand residents. The peak loss occurred in 1998 when almost ten thousand Newfoundlanders packed up and left the province. The loss of people to other locales in Canada and abroad (especially the United States) combined with the lowest birth rate in Canada to cause Newfoundland's overall population to plummet. Its 7 percent decline from the 1996 to the 2001 census represented the lowest growth rate among all of Canada's provinces and territories.

Low immigration figures were another indication that Newfoundland was losing favor as a place to live. In 2001, more than 250,000 immigrants came to Canada but fewer than 500 of them settled in Newfoundland. One particularly dire demographic forecast warns that Newfoundland's current population may shrink from 513,000 in 2001 to 411,000 in 2036.

As Newfoundland's economy has perked up since 1999, the exodus to wealthier provinces has slowed. Estimates for 2002 suggest that the province's net out-migration has been reduced to fewer than one thousand, which would be lower than any year since 1990. Whether this favorable trend will continue over the next few years will depend mainly upon the success of new economic initiatives, according to economist Michael Holden. Energy and mineral development can diversify the economy of Newfoundland and the other depressed maritime provinces, he said in an interview with the *Toronto Star*, creating "great potential for construction and a lot of high-end biochemical, engineering, design and manufacturing positions, if the region can do it right. The opportunity exists and that probably will change the perception and the image of Atlantic Canada."

amount of funds it can raise from income taxes is limited—
Newfoundland already has long had one of the highest basic
income tax rates in Canada. Taxing corporate profits is also
difficult since companies threaten to leave and take all their
jobs with them when faced with increased taxes or even environmental restrictions. Residents also vote with their feet:
Newfoundland experienced a major out-migration during
the 1990s, causing a fall in its overall population. Perhaps
most seriously for the province, it was the most-skilled and
best-educated workers who tended to leave to take jobs in the
churning economies of Ontario, Alberta, and the United
States. Statistics confirm that a significantly higher percentage
of college graduates and doctoral students emigrated from
Newfoundland compared to the general population.

The loss of so many young and educated people makes
Newfoundland's economic recovery all the more difficult.
The collapse of the fishery in 1992 has emphasized the need
to educate a workforce for diverse jobs. The government
would love to attract more high-tech and knowledge-based
industries but companies in these fields need educated workers. Furthermore, as the percentage of the population that is
either under fifteen or over sixty-five increases, the smaller tax
base must support increases in public funds devoted to ex-
pensive health care and social programs. Lower tax revenues
also lead to reductions in public sector employment, such as
teachers, policemen, and government administrators. In the
past the Newfoundland government has borrowed to get
through the tough times but its mounting debt is now a part
of the problem. The province owes creditors more than $5
billion and must divert almost twenty cents out of every tax
dollar collected to pay debt charges.

Balancing Jobs and the Environment

Few people think that it will be easy for Newfoundland to es-
cape its long cycle of job loss, public debt, and population decline. During the last decade Newfoundland has seemed to
sow the seeds of a new political and economic culture, one
centered on extracting oil and other natural resources, attracting high-tech industries, and promoting the area's distinctive culture and heritage, as well as its rugged geography,
for tourism. A consensus has formed that this new economic
model will help prevent the pattern of over-reliance upon
a limited resource, especially fish, that has long hampered

■ Taming the Wind

Because Newfoundland is among the best inhabited places in the world for wind power generation, the government is looking for opportunities to expand this relatively clean energy technology. One recent study of a site in Newfoundland found that on only 7 out of 183 winter days would there be insufficient wind to operate. The Wreckhouse area on the most southwestern tip of Newfoundland Island, near Channel-Port aux Basques, has famously powerful winds—strong enough that gusts once blew a train off its tracks. In the past such high winds were somewhat problematic for wind power generation, since they posed a hazard to the tall machines. Over the last decade, however, wind technology has advanced considerably and turbines no longer need be limited to areas with moderate but steady winds.

One of the reasons Newfoundland is eager to exploit its wind resources relates to Canada's well-publicized commitment to reduce greenhouse gas emissions by 6 percent from 1990 levels by 2010. Wind power produces no such emissions and thus can be an environmentally friendly alternative to coal- or gas-powered electric utilities.

Wind power is not without its own set of environmental considerations, on the other hand. Two of the first proposals for wind power projects in Newfoundland had to be shelved after naturalists raised concerns about their proximity to important bird sanctuaries. Flocks of birds that inadvertently fly into the giant, fast-whirring blades can be cut to pieces. Rita Anderson, president of the Natural History Society in St. John's, said that the environmental group was reluctant to take issue with one project, but it was too close to the millions of seabirds on tiny Baccalieu Island. "Most people would like to see a wind power project," she said. "Our problem is with the location. . . . I'm hopeful they'll find a site."

Newfoundland's development. Exactly how economic demands are balanced with environmental concerns, native rights, and social issues, however, is an ongoing issue for the people of Newfoundland.

A prime example of the inherent challenges is the movement within Newfoundland to protect more of the province's natural environment. Currently less than 2 percent of Newfoundland's total land area has been set aside as protected land. This includes the province's two national parks as well as more than eighty provincial parks and wilderness and ecological reserves. Only one other Canadian province, tiny Prince Edward Island, has a lower percentage of protected land. All the other provinces have protected at least 5 percent of their land, and Quebec, Alberta, and British Columbia exceed 10 percent. A number of proposals are being negotiated that could improve Newfoundland's record in this regard.

New Parks on the Horizon

In 1996 the federal and provincial governments began to negotiate with the Labrador Inuit Association (LIU) to establish a national park in the Torngat Mountains of Labrador. The new park would extend from Saglek Bay almost to Cape Chidley at the northern tip of Labrador and would be larger than the Terra Nova and Gros Morne national parks combined. In 2000 the provincial government and the LIU agreed on interim measures to protect the land from any commercial, industrial, or mineral development. The area of the proposed park contains remnant glaciers and some of the most spectacular coastal fjords in the world.

Since the mid-1970s the federal and provincial governments have also been considering a national park in Labrador's Mealy Mountains, located southeast of huge, saltwater Lake Melville. The area is an untouched wilderness of upland bogs,

■ *Newfoundland's lakes and wildlife areas are drawing increasing numbers of campers and other outdoor enthusiasts.*

■ Officials are considering setting aside a national park within the remote Torngat Mountains in northern Labrador.

boreal forest, wild rivers, and rugged mountains populated by caribou, moose, black bears, and other wildlife. The proposed park has been dogged by failure to resolve issues relating to native land claims and hunting rights; hydroelectric, logging, and mineral development; and a proposal to extend the Trans-Labrador Highway through the area. According to the Innu Nation, "Many people fear that the real motivation for the road is to give the multinational pulp-and-paper companies Abitibi Consolidated and Kruger Ltd. access to the old-growth forests of southeastern Labrador."[34] In 2001 the Canadian and Newfoundland governments, in conjunction with the Innu Nation and the Labrador Inuit Association, agreed on an eighteen-month, $600,000 study on the feasibility of the national park.

A coalition of Newfoundland environmentalists and progressives has also proposed establishing a wilderness reserve in the area of the Main River to the east of Gros Morne National Park. The Main River valley is home to one of the last major old-growth boreal forests on the island and provides an important habitat for a range of Newfoundland animal species on the province's threatened or endangered lists. These include Atlantic salmon, woodland caribou, and Newfoundland marten. National environmental officials recognized the Main's importance in 1991 when it was the first Newfoundland river to be nominated as a Canadian Heritage River, due to its pristine wilderness and outstanding recreational values.

National conservation groups and Newfoundland environmentalists needed to coordinate a decade-long campaign, however, to protect the Main from logging interests. In 2002 the Newfoundland government approved a five-year operating plan for Kruger, owner of Corner Brook Pulp and Paper, to protect only a narrow corridor along the river, leaving most of the watershed open for clearcutting. The decision was met with criticism from environmentalists who point out that modern clearcutting is highly mechanized and provides fewer jobs than a broad-based approach that recognizes the potential for ecotourism, wilderness recreation, and other benefits from forest preservation. "This decision," said Leo White of the Main River Coalition, "is quite simply an affront to all people of the province who care very strongly for our endangered wilderness areas, as well as the long-term health of our communities dependent on forest resources. The Minister of Environment's decision follows in the tradition of pushing our natural resources to the breaking point, in exchange for short-term economic gain."[35]

Toward a Sustainable Future

The debates over oil exploration, mining projects, and parks versus logging underscore how quickly the face of Newfoundland is changing with the times. This sea-dominated land, a place where cod amounted to a virtual currency for centuries, has just within the past few years emerged as a commercial and industrial player in North America and the world. Increasingly its residents are working not at sea but in the information and communications industry, advanced technologies, and retail, trade, and service jobs. More than two dozen customer call centers operate in the province with new ones recently opening in St. John's, Grand Falls–Windsor, and elsewhere, employing upward of four thousand residents. Biotechnology research, especially focusing on marine applications, is making inroads in St. John's—in 2005 the province will host the International Marine Biotechnology Conference, marking the first time the conference is being held in Canada. Book publishing has slowly developed to the point that the province is now putting out sixty new or reprinted titles annually.

St. John's, the province's economic and cultural capital, is a visible example of Newfoundland's revival. Its harbor, which in the late 1990s the Sierra Club

■ *Carol Lake in Labrador City is one of a number of iron ore mines that provides the bulk of Canada's iron.*

rated as the dirtiest in Canada, will soon have a long-overdue cleanup. St. John's and its neighbors, Mount Pearl and Paradise, after years of dumping millions of gallons of raw sewage into the harbor every day, in the fall of 2002 finally agreed on the details of a $93 million sewage treatment project, with most of the funding coming from the provincial and federal governments. Government funds are also backing the construction of an underground Geo Centre at Signal Hill that will showcase Newfoundland's geological history. Beginning in 2004 the galleries, lecture hall, multimedia center, and other attractions of The Rooms will act as a cultural centerpiece for St. John's. The St. John's International Airport has recently undergone a major, $50 million renovation and expansion.

Elsewhere in the province plans are underway to upgrade the Trans-Labrador Highway and expand the network of snowmobile trails, build new hospitals and water treatment plants, and repair and replace wharves and other marine structures. The single most ambitious project, still on the drawing board wish-list at this time, is a potential tunnel beneath the Strait of Belle Isle that would provide a crucial ground link with mainland Canada.

A hardy people long accustomed to the difficulties of living in a rugged environment, the residents of Newfoundland and Labrador face many adjustments as they develop creative solutions to their economic and social challenges. Many will no doubt cast a fond glance back even as they embrace a promising but still uncertain future. As Newfoundland repatriate Michael Crummey recently observed,

> The Newfoundland I came home to is different from the one I carried with me when I was away. Not less itself, but more varied, more expansive. A culture deep enough to accommodate a world of influences without surrendering what makes it unmistakably of this place. Something alive and leaning towards the future. Still, there will always be that ache of loss about Newfoundland for me, a sense of how part of what it was is passing out of our lives for good.[36]

Facts About Newfoundland

Government

- Form: parliamentary system with federal and provincial levels
- Highest official: premier, who administers provincial legislation and regulations
- Capital: St. John's
- Entered confederation: March 31, 1949; tenth and last of the provinces
- Provincial flag: six triangles and an arrow arranged in a Union Jack pattern, with white representing snow and ice, blue the sea, red human effort, and gold societal confidence
- Motto: "Seek ye first the kingdom of God"

Land

- Area: Newfoundland Island: 43,007 square miles (111,390 square kilometers), 27% of province; Labrador: 113,641 square miles (294,330 square kilometers), 73% of province; total: 156,648 square miles (405,720 square kilometers); 4% of total land of Canada; tenth-largest province/territory; rivers and lakes cover approximately 8% of land; total length of coastline is 10,900 miles (17,540 kilometers)
- Boundaries: bounded on the north by the Atlantic's Labrador Sea, on the west by Quebec, on the south by the

Gulf of St. Lawrence, Cabot Strait, and the Atlantic Ocean, and on the east by the Atlantic Ocean

- Bordering bodies of water: Labrador Sea, Atlantic Ocean, Cabot Strait, Gulf of St. Lawrence, Strait of Belle Isle
- National parks: Gros Morne, Terra Nova
- Provincial parks and reserves: 84, encompassing approximately 2,000 square miles (5,000 square kilometers); the largest is Barachoix Pond Provincial Park on Newfoundland Island
- Highest point: Mount Caubvick (also known in Quebec as Mont D'Iberville) in the Torngat Mountains, 5,420 feet (1,652 meters)
- Largest lake: Labrador's Lake Melville, 1,133 square miles (2,934 square kilometers); human-made Smallwood Reservoir, at 2,520 square miles (6,527 square kilometers), is the largest body of fresh water in the province
- Other major lakes and reservoirs: Grand, Red Indian, Gander, Maelpaeg Reservoir
- Longest river: Churchill, 532 miles (856 kilometers)
- Other major rivers: Naskaupi, Eagle, Romaine, Exploits (longest river on Newfoundland Island), Gander
- Time zones: Newfoundland Standard Time (1.5 hours ahead of Eastern Standard Time), Atlantic Standard Time
- Geographical extremes: 46° N to 60° N latitude; 52° W to 67° W longitude

Climate

- Foggiest, snowiest, wettest, windiest, and cloudiest city: St. John's (tops in all categories among major Canadian cities)
- Deadliest hurricane: Independence, which killed an estimated 4,000 British sailors off the coast of Newfoundland Island on September 9, 1775

People

- Population: 512,930 (2001 census), ranking ninth among provinces and territories; 1.7% of Canada's total population of 30,007,094
- Annual growth rate: -7% from 1996 to 2001 (lowest growth rate among provinces and territories)

- Density: 3.3 persons per square mile, compared to Canadian national average of 7.8 (1.3 and 3.0 persons per square kilometer)

- Location: 57% urban; 43% rural; 34% of residents live in the St. John's metropolitan area; 90% of the population is concentrated along the coasts; Labrador accounts for only 5% of the provincial population

- Predominant heritages: British, Irish, French, Scottish, Chinese

- Largest ethnic groups: Innu, Inuit, Mi'kmaq

- Major religious groups: Roman Catholic, Anglican, United Church, Salvation Army

- Primary languages (first learned and still understood): 98% English, 0.5% French, 0.3% Innu, and 1.2% other languages

- Largest metropolitan area: St. John's, population 172,918 (includes Mount Pearl, province's second-largest city), a decrease of 0.7% between 1996 and 2001; nineteenth-largest metropolitan area in Canada

- Other major cities: Corner Brook, Grand Falls–Windsor, Gander, Labrador City–Wabush

- Life expectancy at birth, 3-year average 1995–1997: men 74.4 years; women 80.1; total both sexes 77.2, tenth among provinces and territories (Canadian average: men 75.4; women 81.2; total 78.4)

- Immigration 7/1/2000–6/30/2001: 440, 0.2% of Canadian total of 252,088; ninth-highest of provinces and territories

- Births 7/1/2000–6/30/2001: 4,679

- Deaths 7/1/2000–6/30/2001: 4,531

- Marriages in 1998: 3,117

- Divorces in 1998: 944

Plants and Animals

- Provincial bird: Atlantic puffin

- Provincial game bird: ptarmigan (partridge)

- Provincial flower: pitcher plant

- Provincial tree: black spruce

- Famous breeds: Newfoundland dog, Labrador retriever, Newfoundland pony

- Endangered, threatened, or vulnerable species: Twenty, including Eskimo curlew, piping plover, wolverine, peregrine falcon, woodland caribou, polar bear, short-eared owl, harlequin duck, boreal felt lichen

Holidays

- National: January 1 (New Year's Day); Good Friday; Easter; Easter Monday; Monday preceding May 25 (Victoria or Dollard Day); July 1 or, if this date falls on a Sunday, July 2 (Canada's birthday); 1st Monday of September (Labour Day); 2nd Monday of October (Thanksgiving); November 11 (Remembrance Day); December 25 (Christmas); December 26 (Boxing Day)
- Provincial/Territorial: June 24 (Cabot 500/Discovery Day)

Economy

- Gross domestic product per capita: $21,008 in 1999, twelfth among provinces and territories and 62.1% compared to U.S. average[37]
- Gross provincial product: $12.8 billion at market prices in 2000, ninth among the provinces and territories and 1.3% of gross national product
- Major exports: oil and gas, hydroelectric, newsprint, metals, fish products
- Agriculture: dairy, chickens, eggs, nurseries, produce, fruit, blueberries
- Tourism: heritage sightseeing, whale/iceberg watching, hiking, fishing, birdwatching
- Logging: newsprint, pulp, paper, chipboard
- Manufacturing: food and beverage products, fish processing, clothing, footwear, shipbuilding
- Mining: iron ore (accounting for 93% of the value of the mining industry), gold, limestone/dolomite, nickel, copper, cobalt, zinc, silica

Notes

Introduction: A Wild, Sea-Dominated Place

1. Quoted in "Labrador City," *Yahoo Travel*. http://travel.yahoo.com.

Chapter 1: Geography Is Destiny

2. Harry Thurston, "Newfoundland: The Enduring Rock," *National Geographic*, May 1986, p. 678.

3. Farley Mowat and John de Visser, *This Rock Within the Sea: A Heritage Lost*. Boston/Toronto: Little, Brown, 1968, p. 4.

4. William Pruitt, "Taiga Biological Station Frequently Answered Questions," *Wilds of Manitoba*. www.wilds.mb.ca.

5. David A. Snow, "Seabirds," *Newfoundland and Labrador Tourism*. www.wordplay.com.

6. Robert M. Poole, "Labrador: Canada's Place Apart," *National Geographic*, October 1993, p. 19.

Chapter 2: Humanity Comes Full Circle

7. Thurston, "Newfoundland: The Enduring Rock," p. 685.

8. Ralph T. Pastore, Museum Notes, "The Beothuks," *The Provincial Museum of Newfoundland and Labrador*. www.nfmuseum.com.

9. Will Ferguson, "Day of the Viking," *Maclean's*, July 1, 2002. www.macleans.ca.

10. Bernard Ransom, Museum Notes, "A Century of Armed Conflict in Newfoundland," *The Provincial Museum of Newfoundland and Labrador*. www.nfmuseum.com.

11. Shannon Ryan, "The Framework of Newfoundland History," *STEM~Net*. www.stemnet.nf.ca.

12. J.K. Hiller, Government and Politics, "The Confederation Election of 1869," *Newfoundland and Labrador Heritage*. www.heritage.nf.ca.

Chapter 3: The Struggle for Self-Sufficiency

13. Mark Kurlansky, *Cod: A Biography of the Fish That Changed the World*. New York: Penguin, 1998, p. 132.

14. *Newfoundland and Labrador Heritage*, "Society, Economy and Culture," www.heritage.nf.ca.

15. *Newfoundland and Labrador Heritage*, "Society, Economy and Culture."

Chapter 4: Daily Life

16. Anthony Wilson-Smith, "A Hard Place, Hard to Leave," *Maclean's*, June 11, 2001. www.macleans.ca.

17. Jeff A. Webb, Society, Economy and Culture, "Outports," *Newfoundland and Labrador Heritage*. www.heritage.nf.ca.

18. Poole, "Labrador: Canada's Place Apart," p. 4.

19. *Happy Valley-Goose Bay Homepage*, "Introduction." www.happyvalley-goosebay.com.

20. Phil McCann, Society, Economy and Culture, "Education," *Newfoundland and Labrador Heritage*. www.heritage.nf.ca.

21. Quoted in "Province's Commitment to Health Care Evident in National Expenditure Report," December 16, 1999, *Government of Newfoundland and Labrador*. www.gov.fn.ca.

22. *Guide to the Rock*, "Ice." www3.nf.sympatico.ca.

Chapter 5: Arts and Culture

23. Leslie Brokaw, "Newfoundland's Mission? The Arts," *Boston Globe*, November 10, 2001, p. F1.

24. *Newfoundland and Labrador Heritage*, "The Arts." www.heritage.nf.ca.

25. Catherine Simpson, "Where the Tide Flows: The Crafts of Newfoundland and Labrador," *Craft and Culture Magazine*, Craft Council of Newfoundland and Labrador. www.craftcouncil.nf.ca.

26. Simpson, "Where the Tide Flows."

27. E. Annie Proulx, *The Shipping News*. New York: Touchstone, 1993, p. 47.

28. *Newfoundland and Labrador Heritage*, The Arts, "Literature." www.heritage.nf.ca.

29. Michael Crummey, "'A Time and Place Apart,'" *Maclean's*, August 13, 2001. www.macleans.ca.

30. Brokaw, "Newfoundland's Mission? The Arts," p. F1.

Chapter 6: Current Challenges

31. Kurlansky, *Cod*, p. 192.

32. Quoted in Fred Langan, "How Oil, Nickel, Water Will Turn 'Have-Not' Province into a 'Have,'" *Christian Science Monitor*, March 2, 1998, p. I.1.

33. Quoted in "June 19, 2002 House of Assembly Proceedings," vol. XLIV, no. 28, *Government of Newfoundland and Labrador*. www.gov.nf.ca.

34. *Innu Nation*, "Action Alert: Trans-Labrador Highway," November 17, 1998. www.innu.ca.

35. Quoted in "Coalition Calls on Government and Company to Acknowledge Real Costs of Logging the Main River," August 23, 2002, *Protected Areas Association of Newfoundland and Labrador*. www.nfld.net.

36. Crummey, "'A Time and Place Apart.'"

Facts About Newfoundland

37. *Demographia,* "Canada: Regional Gross Domestic Product Data: 1999." www.demographia.com.

Chronology

1713 French signing of the Treaty of Utrecht cedes control over Newfoundland to the British.

1824 Britain recognizes Newfoundland as a colony.

1829 Shanawdithit, last of the Beothuks, dies from tuberculosis in St. John's.

1855 Newfoundland gains right to elect own government and prime minister, though Great Britain retains final authority.

1858 The first successful transmission of a telegram by transatlantic cable laid on the ocean floor from Newfoundland to Ireland.

1867 Newfoundland chooses not to join with Canada East (Quebec), Canada West (Ontario), Nova Scotia, and New Brunswick as they form Dominion of Canada.

1892 On July 8 a major fire destroys much of St. John's.

1901 Marconi receives first transatlantic radio signal near St. John's.

1919 Alcock and Brown depart from St. John's en route to making the first nonstop flight across the Atlantic, landing almost sixteen hours later in Ireland.

1927 Newfoundland's borders are expanded to include Labrador.

1934 Economic crisis forces Newfoundland to suspend self-government in favor of control by British-appointed officials.

1948 A slim 52 percent majority of Newfoundland voters chooses provincehood over independence.

1949 On March 31, Newfoundland becomes Canada's tenth province.

1992 The Grand Banks cod fishery collapses, putting thousands of Newfoundland fishermen out of work.

1997 Hibernia offshore rig starts producing oil.

2001 Newfoundland celebrates the one thousandth anniversary of Viking settlement at L'Anse aux Meadows.

For Further Reading

Books

Nan Drosdick and Mark Morris, *Atlantic Canada Handbook*. Chico, CA: Moon Publications, 1995. Separate sections on Newfoundland and Labrador in this guide offer basic background on the land, climate, and history as well as travel suggestions.

Mark Kurlansky, *Cod: A Biography of the Fish That Changed the World*. New York: Penguin, 1998. A lively social, historical, and environmental overview.

Farley Mowat and John de Visser, *This Rock Within the Sea: A Heritage Lost*. Boston/Toronto: Little, Brown, 1968. This handsomely designed book on the twilight of outport life combines text by the noted Canadian author Mowat with striking black-and-white photos by de Visser.

Periodicals

Michael Crummey, "'A Time and Place Apart,'" *Maclean's*, August 13, 2001.

Robert M. Poole, "Labrador: Canada's Place Apart," *National Geographic*, October 1993.

Harry Thurston, "Newfoundland: The Enduring Rock," *National Geographic*, May 1986.

Websites

Government of Newfoundland and Labrador (www.gov.nf.ca). The official provincial site offers details on tourism, business, economy, services, and more.

Newfoundland and Labrador Heritage (www.heritage.nf.ca). An informative and beautifully illustrated site that covers the province's history, arts, society, natural environment, and more.

Works Consulted

Books

Wayne Curtis et al., *Frommer's Canada*. New York: Macmillan, 1998. This is an excellent travel guide to the country.

Encyclopedia of Newfoundland and Labrador, 5 vol. St. John's: Newfoundland Book Publishers, 1981–1994. The single most detailed source for everything Newfoundland.

Marion Harrison and Peter Thompson, *Explore Canada: The Adventurer's Guide*. Toronto: Key Porter Books, 1999. Lush photos and up-to-date information for outdoors-people as well as tourists.

Helge Ingstad and Anne Stine Ingstad, *The Viking Discovery of America: The Excavation of a Norse Settlement in L'Anse aux Meadows, Newfoundland*. New York: Facts On File, 2001. This husband-and-wife team of archaeologists describes their groundbreaking site research in the 1960s and provides a detailed history of Viking explorations.

Mark Lightbody, Thomas Huhti, and Ryan Ver Berkmoes, *Canada*. Hawthorn, Australia: Lonely Planet, 1999. An informative and practical guide to the country.

Robert Perkins, *Against Straight Lines*. Boston: Atlantic-Little Brown, 1983. An intrepid modern explorer recounts his canoe trip through the wilderness of northern Labrador.

E. Annie Proulx, *The Shipping News*. New York: Touchstone, 1993. A penetrating novel set in Newfoundland.

Barbara Radcliffe Rogers and Stillman Rogers, *Adventure Guide to Canada's Atlantic Provinces*. Edison, NJ: Hunter Publishing, 1999. A detailed travel book focusing on opportunities for birders, hikers, kayakers, and other outdoor adventurers.

George Whitely, *Northern Seas, Hardy Sailors.* New York: W.W. Norton, 1982. A retired scientist tours his ancestral home by sea and tells gripping stories of Newfoundland's fish trade.

Periodicals

Leslie Brokaw, "Newfoundland's Mission? The Arts," *Boston Globe*, November 10, 2001.

John Demont, "Crisis in the North," *Maclean's*, December 4, 2000.

Department of Finance, Government of Newfoundland and Labrador, *The Economy 2002.* St. John's: Economics and Statistics Branch, 2002.

Fred Langan, "How Oil, Nickel, Water Will Turn 'Have-Not' Province into a 'Have,'" *The Christian Science Monitor*, March 2, 1998.

Michael Macdonald, "Wind Power Project Too Close to Newfoundland Bird Sanctuary, Environmentalists Say," *Canadian Press*, May 8, 2001.

Chris Morris, "Bright Outlook for Atlantic Region Doesn't Compute," *Toronto Star*, June 5, 2001.

Kenneth Taylor, "Puffins," *National Geographic*, January 1996.

Internet Sources

Kevin Cox, "Lower Churchill Project Hits Snag," *Hamilton Spectator*, December 3, 2002. http://spectator. workopolis.com.

Demographia, "Canada: Regional Gross Domestic Product Data: 1999." www.demographia.com.

Guide to the Rock, "Ice." www3.nf.sympatico.ca.

Happy Valley-Goose Bay Homepage, "Introduction." www.happyvalley-goosebay.com.

Innu Nation, "Action Alert: Trans-Labrador Highway," November 17, 1998. www.innu.ca.

Ralph T. Pastore, Museum Notes, "The Beothuks," *Provincial Museum of Newfoundland and Labrador.* www. nfmuseum.com.

Ralph T. Pastore and G.M. Story, "Shawnadithit,"
Colonelby.com. http://colonelby.com.

Protected Areas Association of Newfoundland and Labrador,
"Coalition Calls on Government and Company to Acknowledge Real Costs of Logging the Main River," August
23, 2002. www.nfld.net.

William Pruitt, "Taiga Biological Station Frequently
Answered Questions," *Wilds of Manitoba.*
www.wilds.mb.ca.

Bernard Ransom, Museum Notes, "A Century of Armed
Conflict in Newfoundland," *Provincial Museum of Newfoundland and Labrador.* www.nfmuseum.com

Shannon Ryan, "The Framework of Newfoundland History,"
STEM~Net. www.stemnet.nf.ca.

Catherine Simpson, "Where the Tides Flow: The Crafts of
Newfoundland and Labrador," *Craft and Culture Magazine.* www.craftcouncil.nf.ca.

David A. Snow, "Seabirds," *Newfoundland and Labrador
Tourism.* www.wordplay.com.

The Rooms, "Creating a New Historic Landmark." www.
therooms.ca.

Yahoo Travel, "Labrador City." http://travel.yahoo.com.

Websites

Canada's Digital Collections (http://collections.ic.gc.ca).
Showcases more than four hundred websites celebrating
Canada's history, science, technology, and culture.

The Canadian Encyclopedia (www.thecanadianencyclopedia.
com). This web version of the three-volume printed work
is authoritative and easy to use.

National Archives of Canada (www.archives.ca). An excellent resource for primary documents relating to people,
places, and events.

Maclean's Magazine (www.macleans.ca). Canada's most
popular general interest magazine is a rich source of well-
written articles.

Index

Picture Credits

Cover Photo: © R. Blenkinsopp
© Barrett & MacKay/Newfoundland and Labrador Tourism, 21, 23
© Roderick Beebe/Newfoundland and Labrador Tourism, 92
© Bettman/Corbis, 45, 46
© R. Blenkinsopp, 9, 12, 17, 55, 56, 57
© Canada Tourism Commission, 19
© Canadian Heritage Gallery/National Archives of Canada, 28, 32, 35, 37, 38, 48, 50, 51
© Corel Corporation, 25
© Jeff Fuller, 44
© Hibernia, 81
© Wolfgang Kaehler/Corbis, 31, 59
© J.S. Meres, National Archives of Canada, 34
© Miramax Studios, 74
© M.U.N., 76
© National Library of Canada, 40
© Newfoundland and Labrador dept. of tourism, culture and recreation, 67
© Newfoundland & Labrador Hydro Plant, 85
© Newfoundland and Labrador Tourism, 14, 25, 66, 72
© Parks Canada/Newfoundland and Labrador Tourism, 91
© Carlo Barrera Pezzi/National Archives of Canada, 33
© Ned Pratt Photo/Memorial University, 64, 65
© Pre-Press, 13
© Provincial Archives of NFLD. & Labrador, 42, 43, 62, 87
© Charles E. Rotkin/Corbis, 93
© Helen Parsons Shepherd, 77
© Troy Turner Photo, 71
© Erick Walsh/Craft Council of Newfoundland and Labrador (dolls made by Angela Andrew), 73

About the Author

Mark Mayell is a freelance writer and editor who has authored a half dozen nonfiction books, including *Exploring Canada: Saskatchewan*, as well as numerous magazine articles. He lives with his wife and two children in Wellesley, Massachusetts.